Lift Up Your H

Lift Up Your Hearts!

A Collection of
25 *Khuṭbah* for Friday Prayer
Volume 2

ABDUR RASHID SIDDIQUI

THE ISLAMIC FOUNDATION

Published by
THE ISLAMIC FOUNDATION
Markfield Conference Centre, Ratby Lane,
Markfield, Leicester LE67 9SY, United Kingdom
Tel: (01530) 244944/5, Fax: (01530) 244946
E-mail: i.foundation@islamic-foundation.org.uk
Web site: www.islamic-foundation.org.uk

QURAN HOUSE, P.O. Box 30611, Nairobi, Kenya

P.M.B. 3193, Kano, Nigeria

British Library Cataloguing-in-Publication Data
Siddiqui, A.R.
Lift Up Your Hearts!: A Collection of 25 Khutbah for Friday prayer, Vol.2
1. Islamic sermons, English 2. Jum'ah
I. Title II. Islamic Foundation (Great Britain)
297.3'7

ISBN 0–86037–430–0

Typeset by: N.A. Qaddoura
Cover design by: Nasir Cadir

Printed and bound in Great Britain by
Antony Rowe Ltd., Chippenham, Wiltshire

بسم الله الرحمن الرحيم

Contents

Foreword

Prayers have their own divine dynamics – some come true soon, others keep us in waiting and hope for years and decades. When I contributed my foreword to Brother Abdur Rashid Siddiqui's exhilarating collection of 30 Friday *Khuṭbahs – Lift Up Your Hearts* a couple of years ago, I only prayed that Allah may enable him to complete the count to fifty-two, enabling those who use these *khuṭbahs* to cover a whole year. I was not sure that wish and prayer would be fulfilled that soon. *Al-Ḥamdulillāh*, the second volume containing another twenty-five *khuṭbahs* is seeing the light of day within the span of three years, *Jazāhullāhu khairal jazā'*.

I have read these *khuṭbahs* with keen interest and profound delight. They are not only spiritually elevating but also intellectually stimulating. Brother Siddiqui has covered a vast spectrum of subjects from relationships with Allah *subḥānahū wa Ta'ālā* and the Prophet Muḥammad (*ṣaws*), to relationships with human beings, animals and the environment. He has addressed some of the crucial social and moral issues faced by the Muslims in the West and come up with very informed and realistic suggestions based on the teachings of the Qur'ān and the *Sunnah*. Muslims are not tied to any particular piece of land. The Prophet (*ṣaws*) put it beautifully when he said that the entire landscape of the earth is a mosque unto me. The message is very clear. Every part of the world could be an abode for the Muslims. The only condition is that we must safeguard our identity. It is the direction that is important and the simile of a mosque epitomises that.

The fifty-five *khuṭbahs* now cover almost all major dimensions of Islamic faith and practice. I hope and pray these may be used by the Imāms and speakers as talking points for their presentations not only on the occasion of Friday Prayer but on all relevant occasions. I particularly recommend them to students' Islamic societies to use them for group discussions and personal reflections. May Allah give the author the best of rewards and make this contribution a *ṣadaqah jāriyah* for him and all who use them.

Khurshid Ahmad

Leicester
8 Jumādā al-Thānī 1425
25 July 2004

Introduction

All praise and thanks to Allah *Subḥānahū wa Ta'ālā*[1] Who is the Creator and Sustainer of all the worlds and Who is Most Merciful and Kind. May Allah's blessings be on our beloved Prophet *ṣallallāhu 'alaihi wa sallam*,[2] who is a mercy for the whole world and the benefactor of the human race. I am grateful to our Lord that He enabled me to complete this second volume of Friday *Khuṭbah*. It is gratifying to learn that the first volume was well received and that reviewers have praised my efforts. Many *Khaṭīb* in mosques and universities found them useful and incorporated them in Friday Prayers.

In the earlier volume I included guidelines for *Khaṭībs* who visit universities and deliver *Khuṭbah* which are as follows:

The purpose of *Khuṭbah* is *Tadhkīr* (reminder) and *Tadabbur* (reflection). "O you who believe! When the call is proclaimed to Prayer on Friday hasten earnestly to the Remembrance of Allah" (*al-Jumu'ah* 62: 9). This reminder should exhort the audience towards obedience of Allah and His Prophet (peace be upon him).

It is essentially an *'Ibādah* (Act of Worship). Thus, people are required to listen attentively and talking during the *Khuṭbah* is not allowed.

The Imām follows the precedent set by the Prophet (peace be upon him) and he should be very careful in what he says.

For these reasons and also recognising the fact that our Congregation is composed of different nationalities, different schools of *Fiqh* and followers of different groups actively involved in the revival of Islam, it

1. This phrase praises Allah and will subsequently be abbreviated as (*swt*).
2. It is customary to recite the salutation after the names of prophets. It means "May the peace and blessings of Allah be upon him". In the rest of the book it is abbreviated as "*ṣaws*".

is essential that we do not raise issues that can be seen to advocate one or another specific point of view.

Issues on which we disagree are very few and minor. Instead there is so much to say about those issues on which we do agree.

Islam is a complete Code of Life. It covers spiritual, social, economic, political and legal issues. We can talk about any issue without provoking sectarian feelings. Some issues that we may feel are important but which are also controversial, require a different forum for discussion and debate where the audience can participate and air their views and ask questions of the speakers. Friday *Khuṭbah* is not the right forum to raise controversial issues where people may feel uncomfortable and forced to listen but unable to speak. The creation of such a situation is bad for the Imām as well as for the Congregation.

Such controversial situations have resulted in fights in Mosques in both the UK and abroad. Sectarian killings are rife in certain parts of the Muslim world. We should try to create harmony in the Mosque. We should create a model of a peaceful Muslim society that despite the differences of opinion works harmoniously in presenting the Islamic way of life.

As the time for *Khuṭbah* is very limited, between 15 and 20 minutes, it is essential that we do not exceed this time. Thus, it is not advisable to raise complex issues which need extensive discourse. It is also *sunnah* of the Prophet (peace be upon him) that he kept *Khuṭbah* very short and relevant to the state of the community.

The above guidelines explain how I have tried to restrict my *khuṭubāt* to very basic Islamic teachings within the constraints of time.

Some hints and suggestions as regards the delivery of *khuṭbah* may help those who are not accustomed to public speaking. Nearly everyone feels nervous before having to give a *khuṭbah*. You should have a positive attitude towards this responsibility realising that this is a duty that you are performing for the sake of Allah (*swt*). You should seek His help in accomplishing this task to the best of your ability. The best supplication is the one used by the Prophet Mūsā (peace be upon him) as recorded in *Sūrah Ṭā Hā*:

> *My Lord! Expand me my breast; ease my task for me; and remove the impediment from my speech. So they may understand what I say.*
> (Ṭā Hā 20: 25-28)

Physical preparation can also help. Two or three deep breaths before you start can relax you. If you are relaxed you will feel happier, and you will be behaving more naturally than if you are tense.

As regards the presentation it is important that what you say comes from deep conviction and from your heart so that it can touch the heart of your audience. For this it is recommended not to read from the book but make notes of important points and try to convey this in your own style. Thus you will be able to have eye contact with your audience and can maintain their interest. Even if you have to read do not rush but try to read at a normal speed. Try to make your presentation lively and interesting so that it appeals to your listeners.

I have used many Arabic terms which may be unfamiliar to some listeners, hence always remember to give their English translation and add further explanation if need be. In addition to the references given in the text I have also provided a few references for further reading at the end of some *khuṭubāt*, in order to help readers gain more familiarity with the issues under discussion.

It also seems appropriate to include some *aḥādīth* about the blessings of Friday and the importance of Friday Prayer and *Khuṭbah*. Our beloved Prophet said:

"Friday is the most excellent and distinguished day among the days of the week in the sight of Allah; so much so that it excels both the day of *'Īd al-Fiṭr* and the day of *'Īd al-Aḍḥā* on account of the following five merits: Allah created Adam on Friday; He sent him to the Earth on this day as His vicegerent; Adam died on Friday; there is a blessed time on Friday during which a person is granted by Allah anything lawful and good he prays for and Resurrection will take place on Friday" (Ibn Mājah).

The practice of the Holy Prophet was that he would commence his preparations for Friday on the preceding night and would say: "The night before Friday is a white night and Friday is a bright day" (al-Bayhaqī). It is also narrated from the Prophet (peace be upon him):

"The Friday Prayer is obligatory on every person who believes in Allah and the Last Day; the one who ignores it on account of sport or fun, or trade and business, will be ignored by Allah, Who is Pure and Self-Sufficient" (Dāraquṭnī).

The Prophet (peace be upon him) also gave a dire warning. He said: "People are warned against neglecting Friday Prayer, otherwise Allah will seal their hearts and they will be condemned to negligence (for ever)" (Muslim).

The Prophet (peace be upon him) gave the following advice and guidance for the preparation and offering of Friday Prayer:

The person who has a bath on Friday, puts on the best available clothes, uses perfume if available, and comes for the Prayer, and takes his place quietly without disturbing the people, then offers the Prayer that Allah has destined for him, and sits in perfect silence and peace from the time the Imām arrives till the completion of the Prayer, he will have all his sins committed since the previous Friday expiated on this account (Abū Dā'ūd).

Finally, on Friday, one should spend as much of one's time as possible in remembrance of Allah, recitation of the Holy Qur'ān (especially *Sūrah al-Kahf* and *Sūrah al-Dukhān* – as they are mentioned by the Prophet), asking Allah's forgiveness and doing other good deeds. It is useful to remind the congregation of this valuable guidance.

In the Preface to the first volume of *Lift Up Your Hearts!* my very dear and respected brother Prof. Khurshid Ahmad expressed the hope that I would be able to "produce a second volume so that we have a set of fifty-two *Khuṭubāt* to cover the whole year". By the grace of Allah (*swt*) I was able to compile another twenty-five *Khuṭbāt* to fulfil his wish.

In the first volume my emphasis was on basic Islamic beliefs and practices and some fundamental Islamic concepts. In the present compilation I have tried to cover many moral and social issues from an Islamic perspective as well as problems faced by the Muslim community in the West. So subjects like terrorism, homosexuality, human rights, animal rights and relations with non-Muslims are tackled as well as topics such as our relationship with Allah and His Prophet, social and family life, death and disaster, happiness and despair.

I am most grateful to Prof. Syed Salman Nadvi, who has spared time from his busy schedule, for reading the manuscript and making constructive comments to improve its contents. My grateful thanks are due to Prof. Abdul Raheem Kidwai and Dr. Farid El-Shayyal for their helpful suggestions and advice. I am indebted to Mawlānā Iqbal Ahmad Azami for diligently scrutinising the Arabic text of Qur'ānic verses and *aḥādīth* as well as their translation for accuracy. Mr. Mokrane Guezzou and Mr. Mohamed Rafeek checked and traced the Arabic text of *aḥādīth* that are quoted and I am most grateful for their invaluable help. I have greatly benefited from the editorial suggestions of Mrs. Susanne Thackray. I would also like to thank Mr. Naiem Qaddoura for setting the whole manuscript and the Arabic quotations from the Holy Qur'ān and *aḥādīth* and Mr. Nasir Cadir for the cover design. Last, but not the least, I am most grateful to Dr. Manazir Ahsan for checking the diacritical markings and the Islamic Foundation for undertaking the publication of this book.

I pray to Allah (*swt*) to accept this humble effort. I hope those who have to give *khuṭbah* will find these *Khuṭubāt* useful and use them in their Friday Prayers.

I earnestly pray that Allah (*swt*) in His Gracious Mercy will accept my humble effort and forgive my sins and overlook my shortcomings. May He bless us all with His Mercy and Forgiveness. (*Āmīn*)

Abdur Rashid Siddiqui

Leicester
23 Rabīʿ al-Thānī 1425
11 June 2004

Transliteration Table

Consonants. Arabic

initial: unexpressed medial and final:

ء	’	د	d	ض	ḍ	ك	k
ب	b	ذ	dh	ط	ṭ	ل	l
ت	t	ر	r	ظ	ẓ	م	m
ث	th	ز	z	ع	‘	ن	n
ج	j	س	s	غ	gh	هـ	h
ح	ḥ	ش	sh	ف	f	و	w
خ	kh	ص	ṣ	ق	q	ي	y

Vowels, diphthongs, etc.

Short:	ـَ	a	ـِ	i	ـُ	u
long:	ـَا	ā	ـُو	ū	ـِي	ī
diphthongs:			ـَوْ	aw		
			ـَىْ	ay		

Our Relationship with Allah

وَالَّذِينَ ءَامَنُوٓا۟ أَشَدُّ حُبًّا لِّلَّهِ ... ﴿١٦٥﴾

And those of faith are overflowing in their love for Allah.
(al-Baqarah 2: 165)

Our personal relationship with Allah is one of the foremost and essential qualities that determine our state of *īmān*. Without this relationship there is little substance to our calling ourselves Muslims. Our faith in Allah is the essence of *īmān*. In our *ʿibādah* the inclination of our hearts towards Allah is vital. In our personal ethics consciousness of Allah is crucial. In our dealings with others attainment of Allah's pleasure is the driving force. Thus, all our activities revolve around our having a close and intimate relationship with our Creator.

We can only build a relationship with those whom we know. Yet perceiving the Being of Allah is beyond our comprehension and understanding. However, although our eyes cannot see Him (al-Anʿām 6: 103) we can nonetheless reflect on His attributes to develop our understanding and knowledge of Him. While reading the Qur'ān we come across many of Allah's *(swt)* attributes. Usually with many commands we are reminded that Allah is All Seer and Knower. If any act is prohibited there is a reminder that He is the Most Powerful and Wise. As a servant of Almighty Allah we should try to respond appropriately to His qualities in our lives so that we appreciate the characteristics of our Master. As our Lord is *Rabb* and *Munʿim* (Cherisher and Provider of all bounties) we should be thankful to Him. As He is *Khāliq* (Creator) we should be obedient to Him. As He is *Samīʿ* and *Baṣīr* (All Hearer and Seer) we should seek His help.

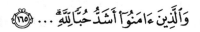

As He is *'Ālim* (Knows Everything) we should trust Him. As He is *Quddūs* (Pure) we should purify ourselves. As He is *'Ādil* and *'Azīz* (Just and Most Powerful) we should be fearful of Him. As He is *Ghafūr* and *Wadūd* (Forgiving and Loving) we should reciprocate by loving Him intensely.

By cultivating this attitude in our lives we are creating the basis of our personal relationship with Allah. The Holy Qur'ān uses very graphic terminology to highlight the warm and intimate bond we should have with Our Master. For example: Those of faith intensely love Allah (al-Baqarah 2: 165); Cling to Allah (al-Ḥajj 22: 78); Run towards Allah (al-Dhāriyāt 51: 50); We [Allah] are nearer to him than his jugular vein (Qāf 50: 16).

The first basis on which we should build up our relationship should be our attitude and actions in acknowledging Allah's bounties bestowed on us. Our hearts, tongues and actions should reflect our sincere thankfulness (*shukr*) to Him. It is common courtesy that if someone helps us we thank them. So why should we neglect to thank Allah Who provides us with generous bounties? If He were to deprive us of them we would be helpless. Once Shaikh Sa'dī, a famous Persian poet and sage, while on his travels was so destitute that he could not afford to buy a pair of shoes. He was very depressed about his condition, then went into a mosque and there he saw a person whose legs had been amputated. He instantly prostrated and thanked Allah for having legs to walk with even if he lacked shoes. We should always look at others who are less fortunate than ourselves and keep remembering and thanking Allah for what He has given us.

Second, we should perform our *'ibādah* (worship) to show our love and devotion to our Creator. Everything in this universe is engaged in praising Allah (*swt*). This is mentioned in several places in the Qur'ān.

يُسَبِّحُ لِلَّهِ مَا فِى ٱلسَّمَـٰوَٰتِ وَمَا فِى ٱلْأَرْضِ ٱلْمَلِكِ ٱلْقُدُّوسِ ٱلْعَزِيزِ ٱلْحَكِيمِ ﴿١﴾

Whatever is in the heavens and on earth declares the praise and glory of Allah – the Sovereign, the Holy One, the Exalted in Might, the Wise.

(al-Jumu'ah 62: 1)

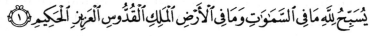

Shaikh Sa'dī in one of his couplets reflected on this as follows:

> A bird does not drink a drop of water
> Until it turns its head towards the sky (to thank Allah, the Creator).

Third, we should try and follow Allah's commands in all affairs. Our lives should be spent in fulfilling our commitment to Allah.

قُلْ إِنَّ صَلَاتِي وَنُسُكِي وَمَحْيَايَ وَمَمَاتِي لِلَّهِ رَبِّ ٱلْعَٰلَمِينَ ﴿١٦٢﴾

Say: "Truly my prayer and my service of sacrifice, my life and my death are (all) for Allah, the Cherisher of the Worlds."
(al-An'ām 6: 162)

This obedience to Allah should, of course, be coupled with *ikhlāṣ* (sincerity). An outward show of piety is fatal. Our public appearances and attitudes should correspond with the private and hidden aspects of our lives.

وَمَآ أُمِرُوٓا۟ إِلَّا لِيَعْبُدُوا۟ ٱللَّهَ مُخْلِصِينَ لَهُ ٱلدِّينَ حُنَفَآءَ ... ﴿٥﴾

And they have been commanded no more than this, to worship Allah, offering Him sincere devotion, being true (in faith).
(al-Bayyinah 98: 5)

Fourth, our love for our Creator should be paramount. We all know what love means. If we love someone we long and yearn to be close to them. We seek to have their pleasure. We constantly think about them and desire to be with them. We are willing to sacrifice everything for them. These are the manifestations of our love in this worldly life. Hence we should at least earnestly love our Creator as well.

Such extreme love and adoration is described as:

وَٱلَّذِينَ ءَامَنُوٓا۟ أَشَدُّ حُبًّا لِّلَّهِ ... ﴿١٦٥﴾

And those of faith are overflowing in their love of Allah.
(al-Baqarah 2: 165)

Imām Ghazālī in his renowned book, *Iḥyā' 'Ulūm al-Dīn*, wrote extensively about love of Allah. He identified many signs by which the state of love between a servant and his Creator can be identified. The following represents a summary of the salient points of his discourse.

1. It is impossible for a heart filled with love not to yearn to meet the object of such desire. Although our desire to meet Him will only be fulfilled once we depart from this world, so we should love death and not abhor it.
2. If we truly love Allah we should be ready to sacrifice everything for Him no matter how much we love other things.
3. If someone loves someone he will constantly remember that person. The sign of one's love for Allah is that we love His *Dhikr* (remembrance).
4. The sign of love is that we should be regular in our recitation of the Holy Qur'ān and our chanting of Allah's praise.
5. If you love someone you will love all those whom he loves. Thus, love of His Prophet (*ṣaws*) is obligatory. "If you love Allah follow me and Allah will love you." (Āl 'Imrān 3: 31)
6. One should not feel sorry and distressed if one loses something. Instead one should remain content and composed at all times. For whatever is destined by Allah will happen.
7. One should find comfort and peace in obedience of Allah.

How can we measure the state of our relationship with Allah? Of course, there are no external measuring instruments to quantify this. Everyone can judge for themselves how close they are to their Creator. As for our ties with Allah, in terms of their increase or decrease, Mawlānā Mawdūdī significantly observed:

> For ascertaining this you need not wait for some vision, miracle and supernatural spectacle. Allah has placed its measure in every heart. You can measure it any time. You should take stock of your life, your activities and your responses. You should ask of yourself, how far you are sincere to the covenant that you have made with Allah by embracing faith.
>
> (*Taḥrīk Awr Kārkun,* p.115)

Let us pray that Allah may give us *tawfīq* (ability) to seek His pleasure through His love and obedience by following the path shown to us by His beloved Prophet (*ṣaws*). His prayers reflect his deep love and devotion to Allah, which we should learn as well.

O Allah! I ask of You Your love, and love of him who loves You. And the love of the deed that will bring me close to Your love.

(*Āmīn*)

Our Relationship with the Prophet

إِنَّآ أَرْسَلْنَٰكَ شَٰهِدًا وَمُبَشِّرًا وَنَذِيرًا ﴿٨﴾ لِّتُؤْمِنُوا۟ بِٱللَّهِ
وَرَسُولِهِۦ وَتُعَزِّرُوهُ وَتُوَقِّرُوهُ ... ﴿٩﴾

We have truly sent you as a witness, as a bearer of glad tidings, and as a warner in order that you (O people) may believe in Allah and His Messenger, that you may assist him and honour him...

(al-Fatḥ 48: 8-9)

The basis of our relationship with the Prophet (*ṣaws*) is part of our *īmān*. By reciting the *Kalimah* (Declaration of Faith) we acknowledge the Prophet Muḥammad as Allah's Messenger. As a Messenger he brought and delivered Allah's (*swt*) message to mankind. There are two aspects of his *Risālah* (Prophethood). First, he delivered the message to his contemporaries living in Arabia. Second, his message was for the whole of mankind till the end of time as he was the last of the glorious chain of prophets. After his death this responsibility of conveying the message was assigned to this *Ummah*. He was sent as a witness unto mankind and this is exactly the task given to the Muslim *Ummah*. The Qur'ān explicitly mentions this in *Sūrah al-Ḥajj*:

هُوَ سَمَّىٰكُمُ ٱلْمُسْلِمِينَ مِن قَبْلُ وَفِى هَٰذَا لِيَكُونَ ٱلرَّسُولُ شَهِيدًا
عَلَيْكُمْ وَتَكُونُوا۟ شُهَدَآءَ عَلَى ٱلنَّاسِ ... ﴿٧٨﴾

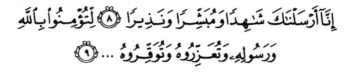

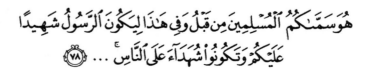

It is He Who named you Muslims, both before and in this (Revelation); that the Messenger may be a witness for you and you be witnesses for mankind...

(al-Ḥajj 22: 78)

As a witness unto mankind, he brought the glad tidings to those who accepted him as Allah's Messenger and believed in him. They attained success in this life and *falāḥ* (salvation) in the Hereafter. For those who rejected his message and followed the path of disobedience there was a dire warning: they could enjoy and indulge in lustful pursuits in this world but in the end they would be the losers and earn eternal damnation.

Believing that the Prophet (*ṣaws*) is Allah's Messenger requires that we should obey him. Obedience to him is on a par with obedience to Allah as the Qur'ān commands: "O you who believe! Obey Allah, and obey the Messenger..." (al-Nisā' 4: 59). Obeying the Prophet is in fact obedience of Allah. He is the one who delivers Allah's message and we have no other means of knowing Allah's commands. Thus, verse 80 of *Sūrah al-Nisā'* explicitly lays down: "He who obeys the Messenger, obeys Allah." We should also take note that this obedience is without reservation. We should accept his commands willingly and not feel any hesitation or scepticism. Allah (*swt*) emphasises this point categorically in the following verses:

فَلَا وَرَبِّكَ لَا يُؤْمِنُونَ حَتَّىٰ يُحَكِّمُوكَ فِيمَا شَجَرَ بَيْنَهُمْ ثُمَّ
لَا يَجِدُوا فِيٓ أَنفُسِهِمْ حَرَجًا مِّمَّا قَضَيْتَ وَيُسَلِّمُوا تَسْلِيمًا ﴿٦٥﴾

But no, by your Lord, they cannot have faith until they make you judge in all disputes between them and find in their hearts any resistance against your decisions, but accept them with the fullest conviction.

(al-Nisā' 4: 65)

وَمَا كَانَ لِمُؤْمِنٍ وَلَا مُؤْمِنَةٍ إِذَا قَضَى ٱللَّهُ وَرَسُولُهُۥٓ أَمْرًا أَن يَكُونَ لَهُمُ ٱلْخِيَرَةُ
مِنْ أَمْرِهِمْ ۗ وَمَن يَعْصِ ٱللَّهَ وَرَسُولَهُۥ فَقَدْ ضَلَّ ضَلَٰلًا مُّبِينًا ﴿٣٦﴾

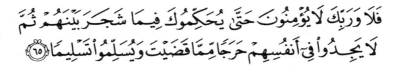

It is not fitting for a believer, man or woman, when a matter is decided by Allah and His Messenger to have an option about their decisions. If anyone disobeys Allah and His Messenger he is indeed on a clearly wrong path.

(al-Aḥzāb 33: 36)

وَمَآ ءَاتَىٰكُمُ ٱلرَّسُولُ فَخُذُوهُ وَمَا نَهَىٰكُمْ عَنْهُ فَٱنتَهُوا۟ ... ﴿٧﴾

So take what the Messenger assigns to you, and deny yourselves that which he withholds from you...

(al-Ḥashr 59: 7)

The same message is given in this *ḥadīth*:

مَانَهَيْتُكُمْ عَنْهُ فَاجْتَنِبُوهُ وَمَاأَمَرْتُكُمْ بِهِ فَافْعَلُوا مِنْهُ مَااسْتَطَعْتُمْ

(البخاري ومسلم)

What I have forbidden to you, avoid: what I have ordered you [to do] do as much as you can.

(Bukhārī and Muslim)

Unlike obedience of national laws in a country where one happens to reside and finding them repulsive but feeling compelled to obey, obedience of the Messenger has to be with full faith and fervour and not half-hearted and perfunctory. One cannot be a believer unless one surrenders oneself fully. It is narrated by ʿAbdullāh ibn ʿAmr ibn al-ʿĀṣ that Allah's Messenger said:

لايُؤمِنُ أَحَدُكُم حَتَّى يَكُونُ هَوَاهُ تَبَعًا لِمَا جِئْتُ بِهِ

(كتاب الحجة)

None of you [truly] believes until his inclination is in accordance with what I have brought.

(*Kitāb al-Ḥujjah*)

Obedience equates with formal adherence of laws and regulations to fulfil the legal requirements of the *Sharīʿah*. However, believers are required to follow the Messenger diligently. This is called *ittibāʿ* which means to follow in the footsteps of others. The instruction given to the believers is: "Say: If you do love Allah follow me; Allah will love you and forgive your sins..." (Āl ʿImrān 3: 31). The circle of *ittibāʿ* is wider than that of *iṭāʿah* (obedience). The latter covers obligatory and compulsory requirements whereas the former covers optional and supererogatory works. Obedience at times may be superficial and lacking sincerity whereas *ittibāʿ* can only be performed with love and devotion. This is illustrated by the Companions' conduct. For example ʿAbdullāh ibn ʿUmar was so strict in following the Prophet (*ṣaws*) that he used to stop and pray where the Prophet happened to have done so. It is narrated that Shaikh Bāyazīd Busṭāmī did not eat watermelon as he did not know whether the Prophet had eaten this fruit and if so how he had eaten it.

Yet a much higher stage of our relationship with the Prophet is his love. Believers should have the utmost respect and love for the Prophet. It is reported that the Prophet (*ṣaws*) said:

لاَيُؤْمِنُ أَحَدُكُمْ حَتَّى أَكُونَ أَحَبَّ إِلَيْهِ مِنْ وَالِدِهِ وَوَلَدِهِ وَالنَّاسِ أَجْمَعِينَ

(البخاري ومسلم)

None of you [truly] believes until you love me more than your parents, children or any other person.

(Bukhārī and Muslim)

This love manifested itself in the lives of the Companions. They were utterly devoted to the Prophet. When he performed *wuḍūʾ* (ablution) the Companions usually collected the used water and sprinkled it on their faces. The Prophet once asked them why they were doing so and they replied because of their love for him (*Mishkāt*). The Prophet (*ṣaws*) once remarked:

وَمَنْ أَحْيَا سُنَّتِي فَقَدْ أَحَبَّنِي وَمَنْ أَحَبَّنِي كَانَ مَعِي فِي الْجَنَّةِ (الترمذي)

Those who love my *Sunnah* (really) love me and those who love me will be in *Jannah* with me.

(Tirmidhī)

Once a father and his son travelled from their village and visited the Prophet (*ṣaws*) and this was probably the only time they met him. They noticed that the top button of his shirt was undone. Thereafter, they always left their top buttons unfastened. When Abū Makhdhūrah embraced Islam the Prophet (*ṣaws*) touched his forehead and blessed him; from then on out of love for the Prophet he never clipped the hairs from his forehead. There are numerous such instances to be found in the lives of the Companions. Love of the Prophet is indeed part of one's *īmān*.

Manifestation of one's love is not just an emotional outpouring but should also be reflected in strict obedience and following of the Prophet's path (*ṣaws*). As he emphasised in the *ḥadīth* quoted above about following his *Sunnah* to those who used the water from his ablution:

مَـــنْ سَرَّهُ أَنْ يُحِبَّ اللّٰهَ ورَسُولَهُ أو يُحبَّهُ اللّٰهُ ورَسُولُه فَلْيَصْدُقْ حَدِيثَهُ
إذَا حَدَّثَ ولْيُؤَدِّ أَمانَتَهُ إذا ائتُمِنَ ولْيُحْسِنْ جِوَارَ مَن جَاوَرَه

(مشكاة المصابيح)

"Those who are pleased to love Allah and His Messenger should always speak the truth and if anything is entrusted to them they should keep it safe and return it to their owners. They should also treat their neighbours well."

(*Mishkāt*)

Today the hearts of the Muslim *Ummah*, *Al-Ḥamdulillāh*, are filled with love and respect for the Prophet (*ṣaws*). People are ready to sacrifice their lives for the sake of safeguarding his honour. Yet not much fervour is shown in obeying his commands and following his path. There are some people who are very particular about some of the Prophet's minor *Sunnah* as regards dress and appearance, yet they neglect his first and foremost *Sunnah* which is *Da'wah*. Allah (*swt*) addressing the Prophet (*ṣaws*) said: "O Prophet! Truly We have sent you as a Witness, a Bearer of Glad Tidings, and a Warner and as one who invites to Allah's grace by His leave and as a Lamp Spreading Light" (al-Aḥzāb 33: 45-46). His greatest *Sunnah*, which he carried out from the day of his messengership until his death, was to invite people to Islam. His parting message on his last *Ḥajj* was: "Those who are here should convey this message to those who are not here." He asked the assembled gathering on the plains of 'Arafāt three times: "Have I conveyed the message?" and the Companions replied "Yes you have". He raised his hand pointing towards the heavens and said: "May Allah be witness to this." This is the *Sunnah* of the Prophet (*ṣaws*) which we have to follow if we truly love him.

May Allah (*swt*) strengthen our bonds of love, affection and respect of the Prophet (*ṣaws*) and guide us to follow his *Sunnah* to the best of our ability.

(*Āmīn*)

Mi'rāj al-Nabī

سُبْحَٰنَ ٱلَّذِىٓ أَسْرَىٰ بِعَبْدِهِۦ لَيْلًا مِّنَ ٱلْمَسْجِدِ ٱلْحَرَامِ إِلَى
ٱلْمَسْجِدِ ٱلْأَقْصَا ٱلَّذِى بَٰرَكْنَا حَوْلَهُۥ لِنُرِيَهُۥ مِنْ ءَايَٰتِنَآ ۚ إِنَّهُۥ
هُوَ ٱلسَّمِيعُ ٱلْبَصِيرُ ﴿١﴾

Glory to (Allah) Who did take His servant for a journey by night from the Sacred Mosque to the Farthest Mosque. Whose precincts We did bless in order that We might show him some of Our signs: for He is the One Who is the Hearer and Beholder.

(al-Isrā' 17: 1)

This verse from *Sūrah al-Isrā'* refers to the Blessed journey on which the Prophet (*ṣaws*) was taken a year before Hijrah. This was one of the most important events in the Prophet's (*ṣaws*) life. This journey was from Masjid al-Ḥarām in Makkah to Masjid al-Aqṣā in Jerusalem. As this journey took place at night it is called *Isrā'* in the Qur'ān, meaning night journey or travelling by night. The journey from Masjid al-Aqṣā to Mala' al-A'lā the seventh heaven is called *Mi'rāj* in *aḥādīth* meaning to ascend or to climb up. The detailed account of *Isrā'* and *Mi'rāj* confirms that this whole event took place during the course of one night.

It is difficult to ascertain the exact date of this important event. Usually events before Hijrah are not easy to pinpoint. There are two reasons for this. First, there was no custom of recording dates at that time. Second, Arabs do not remember the dates of events but rather they remember dates by events. For example, they will say that a certain event took place so many years before or after the Year of the Elephant (when

Abrahah invaded the Ka'bah). With regard to *Mi'rāj*, it is quite certain that it took place after the death of the Prophet's wife Khadījah and before Hijrah. Mawlānā Sayyid Sulaimān Nadwī in *Sīrat al-Nabī* placed it before Hijrah in 12 Nabawī. He cites *Sūrah al-Isrā'* as his proof. The *Sūrah* starts by mentioning the Night Journey and then there are other indications of Hijrah in the *Sūrah* as well. Usually 27th Rajab is widely accepted as the night of *Isrā'* and *Mi'rāj*.

Sometimes questions are raised about whether this incident occurred during the Prophet's (*ṣaws*) sleep or when he was fully awake. About whether the journey was physical or just a dream experience. Usually it is said that *Umm al-Mu'minīn* 'Ā'ishah, Amīr Mu'āwiyah and 'Abdullāh ibn 'Abbās (may Allah be pleased with them) did not believe in physical *Mi'rāj*. However, the view attributed to *Umm al-Mu'minīn* 'Ā'ishah is not based on any authentic narration. Even the views of the others are not to be found in *Ṣiḥāḥ Sittah* – the six most authentic collections of *aḥādīth*.

Commentators have argued that the word *subḥān* (glory) at the start of the verse of *Sūrah al-Isrā'* implies that it was a great event. To see something in a dream is not an extraordinary event that required special mention of Allah's Majesty. Hence this incident is used as a proof of Prophethood. If it were just a dream it would not provide convincing proof. Even unbelievers in Makkah would not have questioned its occurrence or doubted its authenticity.

The overwhelming majority of the Muslim *Ummah* accepts that this took place in full consciousness and with body and soul. In *Fatḥ al-Bārī* Ibn Ḥajar states that *Isrā'* and *Mi'rāj* took place during one night after conferment of Prophethood and when he was awake. This was both a physical and spiritual experience. All *muḥaddithūn*, *fuqahā'* (jurists) and scholars believe this was the case.

Taking into account all narrations of this incident, the details are as follows: one night the Prophet (*ṣaws*) went to Ḥaram and was resting in Ḥaṭīm when Jibrīl came and asked him to mount al-Burāq (a kind of animal smaller than a mule but larger than a donkey). From the Ka'bah the Prophet (*ṣaws*) went to Masjid al-Aqṣā. All the Prophets were gathered there and he led the Prayer. From here the journey started towards heaven. At different stages he met different eminent Messengers. Finally he presented himself to his Lord. At this point the five daily prayers were made obligatory. Then the Prophet (*ṣaws*) returned to Bait al-Maqdis and from there to Masjid al-Ḥarām. Many *aḥādīth* inform us that he was shown *Jannah* and *Jahannam* during his visit.

The next day the Prophet narrated the incident. The unbelievers made fun of it and even those Muslims of weak faith were doubtful. Abū Bakr, without hesitation, acknowledged the Prophet's (*ṣaws*) truthfulness and earned the title *Al-Ṣiddīq* – the Truthful – from that day on.

Some people raise the objection that Allah is not confined to any one specific place, so why should a servant need to be taken to that place. The answer is that whilst it is true that Allah is not stationed in any one specific place, the weakness of human beings is such that they have to be taken to a specific place before Him. Similarly, when Allah wants to talk to human beings He has to use our limited means of communication. Thus, when He has to show His servant His vast and magnificent Kingdom He has to take him there, because a servant cannot see the entire universe as Allah sees it. The same is true of meeting Him. A place has to be chosen where His splendour and manifestation can be concerted. Some ask how he could have been shown *Jannah* and *Jahannam* and people being rewarded and punished, when this judgement has not as yet taken place. The fact is that what he was shown was an allegorical representation of events. For example, mischievous talk is represented as a huge bull coming out of a small hole and unable to return. Adulterers are shown as having good quality meat yet they eat rotten meat. Similarly, punishments for crimes are also demonstrated via parables.

Extraordinary events of this ilk took place in the lives of earlier Messengers.

Such instances are also mentioned in the Holy Qur'ān. For example, about the Prophet Ibrāhīm it is stated:

وَكَذَٰلِكَ نُرِيٓ إِبۡرَٰهِيمَ مَلَكُوتَ ٱلسَّمَٰوَٰتِ وَٱلۡأَرۡضِ
وَلِيَكُونَ مِنَ ٱلۡمُوقِنِينَ ٧٥

So also We show Ibrāhīm the power and the laws of the heavens and the earth, that he might (with understanding) have certitude.

(al-An'ām 6: 75)

The Prophet Ibrāhīm (peace be upon him) was also shown how Allah gives life to the dead (al-Baqarah 2: 260). The encounter between the Prophet Mūsā (peace be upon him) and Khiḍr as narrated in *Sūrah al-Kahf* gave him glimpses of insight into Allah's knowledge of the future and explanations about apparently unjust acts and events. Again, when one of the Prophets passed through a village in ruins and exclaimed: "How shall Allah bring it (ever) to life after its death?" Allah put him to sleep for a hundred years and then revived his donkey which was just a skeleton of bones (al-Baqarah 2: 259).

The reason for showing the power and might of Allah as well as glimpses of the Unseen is to give certitude to His Messengers. They are required to testify the truth about the Unseen and thus they can convince their people that they have witnessed the Unseen and are convinced of what they ask people to believe.

After showing His Messenger His mighty Kingdom in heaven and earth, Allah (*swt*) revealed the blueprint of the Islamic State soon to be established in Madinah. Verses 23-40 give a 14-point policy statement on which the Islamic State was to be established. This task of the Prophethood was well illustrated by ʿAllāmah Iqbāl, the poet-philosopher of Islam, by quoting the following episode. Mawlānā ʿAbdul Quddūs Gangohī was an eminent mystic of the Indian sub-continent. After narrating the story of *Mʿirāj,* he observed: "I swear by God that if I had reached that point, I should never have returned." To which Iqbāl commented:

> In the whole range of Sufi literature it will be probably difficult to find words which, in a single sentence, disclose such an acute perception of psychological difference between the prophetic and mystic type of consciousness.

This illustrates the difference between a Prophet and a mystic. The ultimate aim of a mystic is to attain union with God while the task of the Prophet is to lead his *Ummah* and accomplish his mission in the world. As Iqbāl says:

> The prophet's return is creative. He returns to insert himself into the sweep of time with a view to controlling the forces of history, and thereby to create a fresh world of ideals.
>
> (*The Reconstruction of Religious Thought in Islam,* p.124)

The experience the Prophet had during *M'irāj* was, by the mercy of Allah, bestowed upon Muslims in the form of obligatory Prayers. The Prophet (*ṣaws*) has said that Prayers is *M'irāj* of a believer. Since *M'irāj* which the Prophet (*ṣaws*) had, could not be attained by us, still we can share the experience of nearness to Allah in our Prayers.

The blessed land from where the Prophet (*ṣaws*) ascended to the heavens has great importance for Muslims. It was the first *Qiblah* before Allah changed it to the Ka'bah, Masjid al-Ḥarām. As the verse from *Sūrah al-Isrā'* highlighted its precincts are blessed by Allah. It was the place where the Prophet led the congregation of Messengers and Prophets in Prayer. It was the place from where he was lifted up to heaven. This is now where the Masjid Qubbat al-Ṣakhrah – Dome of the Rock – stands. The Ḥaram al-Sharīf includes the Masjid al-Aqṣā.

It is very sad that Muslims lost control of this third holiest place in 1967. The Israelis then tried to destroy it, in 1969 and 1980 and then again in 1982. They started excavations underneath to destabilise its foundations. The Jewish plan is to destroy Ḥaram al-Sharīf and build their Temple in its place. The Zionists with the support of the United States are inflicting untold misery and devastation on the Palestinian people. The Muslim States watch all this and call conferences and pass resolutions without lifting a finger to redress this situation. While the Muslim masses protest and collect funds for relief, they are unable to help in any other way. If only we could be united and could make a collective effort we could liberate the Holy Land of Palestine.

Let us pray to Allah (*swt*) that He may grant us the power and resources and unite us to regain the Blessed Land of Palestine.

(*Āmīn*)

Justice

إِنَّ ٱللَّهَ يَأْمُرُ بِٱلْعَدْلِ وَٱلْإِحْسَٰنِ وَإِيتَآئِ ذِى ٱلْقُرْبَىٰ وَيَنْهَىٰ عَنِ
ٱلْفَحْشَآءِ وَٱلْمُنكَرِ وَٱلْبَغْىِ ۚ يَعِظُكُمْ لَعَلَّكُمْ تَذَكَّرُونَ ﴿٩٠﴾

Allah commands justice, the doing of good, and liberality to kith and kin, and He forbids all shameful deeds and wickedness and rebellion: He instructs you, that you may receive admonition.

(al-Naḥl 16: 90)

The verse from *Sūrah al-Naḥl* that I have just recited is universally quoted by imāms throughout the world in their Friday *Khuṭbah.* It was not used as part of the Prophet's (*ṣaws*) *Khuṭbah* nor did the Companions recite it. This tradition was started by ʿUmar ibn ʿAbdul ʿAzīz, the Umayyad *Khalīfah*, who is considered by some to be the fifth rightly-guided *khalīfah*. After years of civil war among the Muslims during the Umayyad period it became a tradition to include curses and abuse on opposing Muslim factions. ʿUmar ibn ʿAbdul ʿAzīz asked all imāms to recite this verse and refrain from cursing others. This was such agreeable advice that it gained widespread support across the Muslim *Ummah*.

The verse from *Sūrah al-Naḥl* is indeed a very comprehensive set of instructions. The first commandment from Allah is to do justice (*ʿadl*). Justice is the fundamental injunction imposed on human beings. In the Holy Qur'ān several words are used to express the notion of justice. The word *ʿadl* (justice) is used in this verse; whereas in *Sūrah al-Ḥadīd* the word used is *qisṭ* (equity) and in *Sūrah al-Raḥmān* the term *mīzān* (balance) is mentioned. It is evident from any study of the Qur'ān that the specific purpose for sending down prophets and scriptures was that there should be justice in society.

لَقَدْ أَرْسَلْنَا رُسُلَنَا بِٱلْبَيِّنَٰتِ وَأَنزَلْنَا مَعَهُمُ ٱلْكِتَٰبَ وَٱلْمِيزَانَ لِيَقُومَ ٱلنَّاسُ بِٱلْقِسْطِ ... ﴿٢٥﴾

Indeed We sent Our Messengers with clear signs and sent down with them the Book and the Balance (of Right and Wrong) so that people might uphold justice.

(al-Ḥadīd 57: 25)

In another place it is stated that the whole universe has been established on the basis of harmonious balance. Hence human beings should not transgress and create imbalance.

وَٱلسَّمَآءَ رَفَعَهَا وَوَضَعَ ٱلْمِيزَانَ ﴿٧﴾ أَلَّا تَطْغَوْا۟ فِى ٱلْمِيزَانِ ﴿٨﴾ وَأَقِيمُوا۟ ٱلْوَزْنَ بِٱلْقِسْطِ وَلَا تُخْسِرُوا۟ ٱلْمِيزَانَ ﴿٩﴾

And the Firmament has He raised high, and He has set up the Balance (of justice), in order that you may not transgress (due) balance. So establish the weight with equity, and do not make the balance deficient.

(al-Raḥmān 55: 7-9)

Thus, we see that the establishment of justice and equity within human society is in consonance and harmony with what Allah has already established in the Universe.

The concept of justice, equity and fair dealing is one of the basic tenets of morality that is imbibed in all human beings. Regardless of religion, race or nationality human beings throughout history admire and praise justice and fair play and despise injustice and iniquity. So why do people perpetrate injustice on others? What motivates them to transgress the path of fairness and oppress others? Allah (*swt*), Who knows human weaknesses, identified them in the Glorious Qur'ān as follows:

يَٰٓأَيُّهَا ٱلَّذِينَ ءَامَنُوا۟ كُونُوا۟ قَوَّٰمِينَ بِٱلْقِسْطِ شُهَدَآءَ لِلَّهِ وَلَوْ عَلَىٰٓ أَنفُسِكُمْ
أَوِ ٱلْوَٰلِدَيْنِ وَٱلْأَقْرَبِينَ ۚ إِن يَكُنْ غَنِيًّا أَوْ فَقِيرًا فَٱللَّهُ أَوْلَىٰ بِهِمَا ۖ
فَلَا تَتَّبِعُوا۟ ٱلْهَوَىٰٓ أَن تَعْدِلُوا۟ ۚ وَإِن تَلْوُۥٓا۟ أَوْ تُعْرِضُوا۟ فَإِنَّ ٱللَّهَ
كَانَ بِمَا تَعْمَلُونَ خَبِيرًا ﴿١٣٥﴾

You who believe! Stand out firmly for justice, as witnesses to Allah, even against yourselves, or your parents, or your relations, and whether it is (against) the rich or poor: for Allah can protect both. Follow not the lusts (of your hearts), lest you sway, and distort (justice) or decline to do justice; verily Allah is well acquainted with all that you do.

(al-Nisā' 4: 135)

The reason why injustices manifest themselves is because people are swayed more by their self-interest than by their admiration for justice. If decisions affect their personal lives or those of their parents or close relations, people are inclined to unjustly defend their position. The other motive influencing human decisions is the status of the parties concerned in a dispute. Often people tend to favour the rich and influential in society and thus stray from the path of justice. Conversely, sometimes out of pity for the poor people decide to favour them. Both attitudes are wrong, as Allah is the best of Protectors. If we were truly conscious at all times that Allah is watching over us then we would not be unduly swayed by self-interest or favouritism.

The other motive that diverts people from the path of justice is also identified by Allah in this verse:

يَٰٓأَيُّهَا ٱلَّذِينَ ءَامَنُوا۟ كُونُوا۟ قَوَّٰمِينَ لِلَّهِ شُهَدَآءَ بِٱلْقِسْطِ ۖ
وَلَا يَجْرِمَنَّكُمْ شَنَـَٔانُ قَوْمٍ عَلَىٰٓ أَلَّا تَعْدِلُوا۟ ۚ ٱعْدِلُوا۟
هُوَ أَقْرَبُ لِلتَّقْوَىٰ ۖ وَٱتَّقُوا۟ ٱللَّهَ ۚ إِنَّ ٱللَّهَ خَبِيرٌۢ
بِمَا تَعْمَلُونَ ﴿٨﴾

You who believe! Stand out firmly for Allah, as witnesses to fair dealing, and let not the hatred of others to you swerve you to wrong and to depart from justice. Be just: that is nearer to piety and fear Allah for Allah is well acquainted with all you do.

(al-Mā'idah 5: 8)

Enmity towards opponents creates feelings of hatred and revenge. Throughout history this has led people to depart from the course of justice and fair dealing, to treat others with contempt and to undermine their rights. "My nation right or wrong" has even gained currency among civilised nations. The Islamic teaching is that Muslims should stand firm and be witnesses to the truth. It is reported that once the Prophet (*ṣaws*) said:

أُنْصُرْ أَخَاكَ ظَالِمًا أَوْ مَظْلُومًا فَقَالَ رَجُلٌ يَا رَسُولَ اللّٰه أَنْصُرُهُ إِذَا كَانَ مَظْلُومًا أَفَرَأَيْتَ إِذَا كَانَ ظَالِمًا كَيْفَ أَنْصُرُهُ قَالَ تَحْجُزُهُ أَوْ تَمْنَعُهُ مِنْ الظُّلْمِ فَإِنَّ ذَلِكَ نَصْرُهُ

(البخاري ومسلم)

"Help your brother whether he is oppressor or being oppressed." One of the Companions was surprised to hear this and asked: "Of course I can help the oppressed but how can I help the oppressor?" The Prophet (*ṣaws*) said: "By refraining him from committing oppression. This is (in fact) helping him."

(Bukhārī and Muslim)

During the last century when India was ruled by the British, a dispute arose among local Muslims and Hindus about a piece of land adjacent to the site of the Mosque in the city of Kandhala (District Muzaffarnagar, United Province). The Muslims started building the Jāmiʿ Mosque declaring the land to be the property of the Mosque. Whereas the Hindus claimed that this piece of land was part of their ancient Temple. The case went to the Court and its hearing continued for several years. As there was no documentary evidence to prove ownership of the land, the English District Magistrate found it impossible to settle the dispute. In the end, he decided to consult the Hindus and Muslims separately. He asked the Muslims to identify any Hindu who would testify that this plot of land belonged to the Mosque. The Muslims replied that as this was a religious matter they doubted if any Hindu would give impartial evidence. The Magistrate put the same question to the Hindus. They said there was a Muslim saintly person in the city who they believed would never lie. He was Mawlānā Maḥmūd Bakhsh Kāndhalawī (d.1939). This respected *'ālim* (learned person) was summoned to the court where a multitude of people from both communities was assembled. When he was asked about ownership of the piece of land, he without hesitation and fear declared that this land belonged to the Hindus and that the Muslims were wrong in their claim, thus upholding the Qur'ānic injunction of being a witness to truth and upholding the commandment of just and fair dealing. The Magistrate's decision allocated the land to the Hindus who built a Temple there. Our history records many such instances of upright people.

In *Sūrah al-Nisā'* there is a specific decree:

إِنَّ ٱللَّهَ يَأْمُرُكُمْ أَن تُؤَدُّوا۟ ٱلْأَمَـٰنَـٰتِ إِلَىٰٓ أَهْلِهَا وَإِذَا حَكَمْتُم بَيْنَ ٱلنَّاسِ أَن
تَحْكُمُوا۟ بِٱلْعَدْلِ ۚ إِنَّ ٱللَّهَ نِعِمَّا يَعِظُكُم بِهِۦٓ ۗ إِنَّ ٱللَّهَ كَانَ سَمِيعًۢا بَصِيرًا ﴿٥٨﴾

Allah commands you to deliver whatever you have been entrusted with to their rightful owners, and whenever you judge between people, judge with justice. Most excellent is what Allah exhorts you to do. Allah hears all and sees all.

(al-Nisā' 4: 58)

Sayyid Quṭb in his monumental commentary, *Fī Ẓilāl al-Qur'ān*, explained this verse in a lucid and clear way. He wrote:

> The order to maintain justice is stated in the most general terms so as to make it obligatory between all people. It does not mean that justice should be confined to Muslims only, or to dealings between them and the followers of earlier Divine religions alone. Justice is due to every individual human being. The requirement to maintain

> justice only takes into account the fact that people are human beings, and that alone qualifies them for just treatment. Hence, justice should be extended to all: believers and non-believers, friends and enemies, white and coloured, Arabs and non-Arabs, etc. The Muslim community, whenever it exercises power, is responsible for maintaining justice between them all.
>
> (*In the Shade of the Qur'ān,* Vol.3, p.194)

Justice demands that all human beings should be treated fairly. But this does not imply that there should always be equality among them in all matters. Of course there are some basic civil rights where there is equality among all citizens, for example the right to participate in elections. But there will be inequality in the remuneration of those who work in different fields or positive discrimination in favour of the disabled and oppressed. We know attempts to create artificial equality in certain states failed miserably. The Islamic teachings are such that everyone should have equal political, economic and social rights and everyone should be treated justly. The calamity in our society is that many people are stripped of their lawful rights and treated unjustly.

It is sad that even Muslims are forgetful of their responsibility to uphold justice in their personal and public lives. There is wilful disregard of justice, equity and fair dealing in many Muslim countries. Their rulers flagrantly oppress their own citizens and plunder their rights. Muslims who should have been witnesses for Allah and leaders in upholding the standard of justice in the world are now among the worst perpetrators in establishing unjust regimes.

May Allah (*swt*) guide us to remain firm on the path of justice as this is the true path of piety and grace.

(*Āmīn*)

— KHUṬBAH THIRTY-FIVE —

Iḥsān

ٱلَّذِينَ يُنفِقُونَ فِي ٱلسَّرَّآءِ وَٱلضَّرَّآءِ وَٱلْكَٰظِمِينَ ٱلْغَيْظَ
وَٱلْعَافِينَ عَنِ ٱلنَّاسِ ۗ وَٱللَّهُ يُحِبُّ ٱلْمُحْسِنِينَ ﴿١٣٤﴾

Those who spend (freely) in prosperity or in adversity; who restrain anger and pardon (all) persons – for Allah loves those who do good deeds.

(Āl ʿImrān 3: 134)

Iḥsān is the quality in human beings that beautifies their character. The word *iḥsān* is derived from *ḥasan* meaning benevolence, good acts, politeness, sympathy, generosity, tolerance and consideration. It is used extensively in the Holy Qur'ān and the *aḥādīth* of the Prophet (*ṣaws*) as a desirable quality of believers. In brief, *iḥsān* is to do an act or treat others in the best possible way.

Whereas justice (*ʿadl*) requires we deal with others fairly, *iḥsān* requires we should deal with people generously. We should not try to extract our rights from others but instead perhaps forego them so as to create better relations. Similarly, we should try to give others more than their due so as to enjoy harmonious relations in society. Such an attitude of generosity, politeness and benevolence perhaps will win the hearts of others.

The verse I have just recited identifies several qualities of *muḥsinīn* (benevolent people). The first and foremost is *infāq* (spending in charity). This means that they are not miserly and attached to their wealth but rather give generously to others and help in alleviating poverty and looking after the downtrodden and destitute. Whereas it is comparatively easy to give away in charity when one has plenty, the quality of *muḥsinīn* is that they are equally generous when they themselves face adversity. Their other characteristic is that of a gentle temperament, which helps them in restraining anger. They control their temper and do not become violent and abuse others in a fit of anger. Their third important quality is their forgiving nature. They are ready to pardon the shortcomings of others rather than embark upon taking revenge. In other places in the Qur'ān qualities like *ṣabr* (patience) and *taqwā* (God-consciousness) are also mentioned. (Sūrah al-Naḥl 16: 127-128.)

Therefore, *iḥsān* is a very comprehensive term. It covers all types of good behaviour and concern for other fellow human beings. It means that a person uses his wealth and his capabilities for the good and welfare of the society in which he lives. The best explanation of *iḥsān* is given by the Prophet (*ṣaws*) in a very important *ḥadīth* known as *Ḥadīth* Jibrīl. Once Archangel Jibrīl came in human form and asked several questions about the tenets of Islam in order to teach the Companions about the *Dīn*. One of his questions to the Prophet (*ṣaws*) was:

فَأَخْبِرْنِي عَنِ الْإِحْسَانِ قَالَ أَنْ تَعْبُدَ اللَّهَ كَأَنَّكَ تَرَاهُ فَإِنْ لَمْ تَكُنْ تَرَاهُ فَإِنَّهُ يَرَاكَ

(مسلم)

"Tell me about *al-iḥsān*." The Prophet (*ṣaws*) answered: "It is that you worship Allah as if you see Him, and while you see Him not yet truly He sees you."

(Muslim)

In this *ḥadīth* the Prophet (*ṣaws*) did not give a dictionary-type meaning of *iḥsān*. Instead, he explained the real motivation behind the performance of one's duty. One should always be conscious that Allah is watching over all one's actions and one's real motive should be to attain Allah's pleasure and avoid His disapproval. This brings about a purity of heart. It ensures that a person is concerned with the quality of his deeds and not the mere performance of his obligations. Thus, the effect of feeling that one sees Allah results in the performance of acts of worship in the best possible way. Such a person will be filled with awe and admiration for his Lord and he will be fully absorbed in his devotion. However, this is a difficult level for everyone to reach. The lower level is to realise that our Lord is watching us and that we are in His august presence. Thus, the presence of either level of *iḥsān* results in worship of Allah in an excellent manner.

Mawlānā Manẓūr Nuʿmānī made a very perceptive observation in this respect:

> Often it is maintained that it applies exclusively to Prayers. It is said that only Prayer is required to be offered with full humility and devotion. But the words of the *ḥadīth* do not justify this. It speaks of *taʿabbud* which denotes absolute worship and obedience. Thus, there is no justification for limiting the Prophet's observation to Prayers. Moreover, in another version of this *ḥadīth* the word *takhshā* has been used in place of *taʿbud*, which, when translated into English reads: "*Iḥsān* means that you fear Allah as if you see Him." Yet another version has it that "*Iḥsān* means that you perform every act for the sake of Allah in such a way as if you are seeing Him." Both these accounts make clear that *iḥsān* covers the entire range of living and doing. Its pith and substance is that every act of worship and obedience should be performed and all commands carried out and the prospect of Final Reckoning dreaded as if our Lord is present before us and watching our every act and movement.
>
> (*Maʿārif al-Ḥadīth,* Vol.1, p.69)

Thus, *iḥsān* is not confined to acts of worship only but it requires that everything should be done to the best of one's ability. Attaining the status of *iḥsān* requires excellence in the performance of all deeds. The Prophet (*ṣaws*) even advised us to use a very sharp knife for slaughter so as not to inflict more pain than is necessary on the animal. The same should be the practice in performing all other actions.

As *iḥsān* deals with purification of the inner self, it is the essence of Islamic *tazkiyah* teachings. Thus, *iḥsān* is the basis of Islamic *taṣawwuf* (Sufism). However, the purity and spontaneity of the Companions and earlier followers of the path of *iḥsān* became contaminated with Greek, Persian and Hindu mysticism and ended up as an un-Islamic mixture of questionable practices.

The advice given by Shāh Walīullāh in his books *al-Fawz al-Kabīr* and *Ḥujjatullāh al-Bālighah* provides us with the best course of action to be followed:

> To acquire this status [of *iḥsān*] a person should always express his humility and his helplessness and his utter dependence on Allah. Allah's heights should always be in his consciousness. He should try to control his carnal self. He should not make this world his aim in life but should consider it as a means of achieving the higher status of *iḥsān*.

How should we create such thinking? How can we change the direction of our lives? Shāh Walīullāh took this *ḥadīth* of the Prophet (*ṣaws*) as his basis:

> An hour of reflection and contemplation is better than sixty years of *'Ibādah* (worship) without reflection and contemplation.

He identified several areas of reflection. Yet reflection cannot be about the "person" of Allah (*swt*) as this is outside human beings' capacity. We are unable to perceive Him. We cannot comprehend Allah's person (*Dhāt*). We can only know Him by His qualities and attributes (*ṣifāt*): His Bounties, His Mercy, His Wisdom and His Creation. Shāh Walīullāh recommended that we reflect on specific verses of the Qur'ān and *aḥādīth* for this purpose. These verses should be repeated often and time should also be set aside to reflect on their meaning. Some of the verses he recommended are as follows:

وَهُوَ مَعَكُمْ أَيْنَ مَا كُنتُمْ ... ﴿٤﴾

And He is with you wherever you are.

(al-Ḥadīd 57: 4)

وَمَا يَعْزُبُ عَن رَّبِّكَ مِن مِّثْقَالِ ذَرَّةٍ فِي ٱلْأَرْضِ وَلَا فِي ٱلسَّمَآءِ
وَلَآ أَصْغَرَ مِن ذَٰلِكَ وَلَآ أَكْبَرَ إِلَّا فِي كِتَٰبٍ مُّبِينٍ ﴿٦١﴾

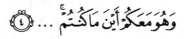

And not so much as the weight of an atom in the earth or heaven is hidden from your Lord, neither anything smaller than that or greater. All things are recorded in a manifest Book.

(Yūnus 10: 61)

إِنَّ ٱللَّهَ عَلَىٰ كُلِّ شَيۡءٖ قَدِيرٞ ﴿٢٠﴾

Indeed Allah has power over all things.

(al-Baqarah 2: 20)

وَنَحۡنُ أَقۡرَبُ إِلَيۡهِ مِنۡ حَبۡلِ ٱلۡوَرِيدِ ﴿١٦﴾

And We are nearer to him than his jugular vein.

(Qāf 50: 16)

وَإِن يَمۡسَسۡكَ ٱللَّهُ بِضُرّٖ فَلَا كَاشِفَ لَهُۥٓ إِلَّا هُوَۖ وَإِن يَمۡسَسۡكَ بِخَيۡرٖ
فَهُوَ عَلَىٰ كُلِّ شَيۡءٖ قَدِيرٞ ﴿١٧﴾ وَهُوَ ٱلۡقَاهِرُ فَوۡقَ عِبَادِهِۦۚ وَهُوَ ٱلۡحَكِيمُ ٱلۡخَبِيرُ ﴿١٨﴾

If Allah touches you with affliction none can remove it but He; if He touches you with happiness, He has power over all things. He is the Irresistible (watching) from above over His servants and He is the Wise, All-Knowing.

(al-Anʿām 6: 17-18)

Let us pray that Allah in His Infinite Mercy gives us *tawfīq* (ability) to make sincere efforts to follow the path of *iḥsān* and attain this coveted status and thereby achieve His pleasure.

(Āmīn)

Obscenity and Evil Deeds

يَٰٓأَيُّهَا ٱلَّذِينَ ءَامَنُواْ لَا تَتَّبِعُواْ خُطُوَٰتِ ٱلشَّيۡطَٰنِۚ وَمَن يَتَّبِعۡ خُطُوَٰتِ ٱلشَّيۡطَٰنِ
فَإِنَّهُۥ يَأۡمُرُ بِٱلۡفَحۡشَآءِ وَٱلۡمُنكَرِۚ وَلَوۡلَا فَضۡلُ ٱللَّهِ عَلَيۡكُمۡ وَرَحۡمَتُهُۥ مَا زَكَىٰ مِنكُم
مِّنۡ أَحَدٍ أَبَدٗا وَلَٰكِنَّ ٱللَّهَ يُزَكِّي مَن يَشَآءُۗ وَٱللَّهُ سَمِيعٌ عَلِيمٞ ﴿٢١﴾

O you who believe! Follow not Satan's footsteps. If any of you will follow the footsteps of Satan, he will (but) command what is shameful and evil. And were it not for the grace and mercy of Allah on you, not one of you would ever have been pure: but Allah does purify whom He pleases and Allah is One Who hears and knows (all things).

(al-Nūr 24: 21)

It is the mercy of Allah (*swt*) that has provided human beings with guidance as to how to spend our time on this planet. We instinctively know what is good and what is bad. At the same time we have been given the choice of following either the path of piety or the path of sin. That this choice is available to us is made explicit in the Glorious Qur'ān:

إِنَّا هَدَيۡنَٰهُ ٱلسَّبِيلَ إِمَّا شَاكِرٗا وَإِمَّا كَفُورًا ﴿٣﴾

We showed him the way; whether he be grateful or ungrateful (rests on his will).

(al-Dahr 76: 3)

Each human being has been given the potential to do good or evil deeds.

وَنَفْسٍ وَمَا سَوَّىٰهَا ﴿٧﴾ فَأَلْهَمَهَا فُجُورَهَا وَتَقْوَىٰهَا ﴿٨﴾

By the soul, and the proportion and order given to it; and its enlightenment as to its wrong and its right.

(al-Shams 91: 7-8)

Thus, it is left to each individual to decide whether to purify his soul with righteous deeds or to corrupt it with obscenity and indecency.

The story of Adam and Eve and their fall from grace is told in several places in the Qur'ān. It narrates how both were tricked by Satan into disobeying Allah. When they were forgiven by Allah, the Merciful, and sent down to earth to fulfil their mission of *Khilāfah* for which they were created, Satan sought Allah's respite to continue to misguide them, leading them astray and tempting them to obscenity and disobedience. Allah granted him his request and Satan vowed to lead Adam and his progeny away from the path of righteousness.

قَالَ فَبِمَآ أَغْوَيْتَنِى لَأَقْعُدَنَّ لَهُمْ صِرَٰطَكَ ٱلْمُسْتَقِيمَ ﴿١٦﴾ ثُمَّ لَءَاتِيَنَّهُم مِّنۢ بَيْنِ
أَيْدِيهِمْ وَمِنْ خَلْفِهِمْ وَعَنْ أَيْمَٰنِهِمْ وَعَن شَمَآئِلِهِمْ ۖ وَلَا تَجِدُ أَكْثَرَهُمْ شَٰكِرِينَ ﴿١٧﴾

He said: "Because You have thrown me out of the way, lo! I will lie in wait for them on Your Straight Path. Then I will assault them from the front and from the back, from their right and their left. You will not find in most of them gratitude for Your mercy."

(al-A'rāf 7: 16-17)

To help human beings remain on the Straight Path and lead a life of piety, Allah (*swt*) sent His messengers to provide guidance.

قُلْنَا ٱهْبِطُوا۟ مِنْهَا جَمِيعًا ۖ فَإِمَّا يَأْتِيَنَّكُم مِّنِّى هُدًى فَمَن تَبِعَ هُدَاىَ
فَلَا خَوْفٌ عَلَيْهِمْ وَلَا هُمْ يَحْزَنُونَ ﴿٣٨﴾

We said: "Get down all from here; and if, as is sure, there comes to you guidance from Me, whosoever follows My guidance, on them shall be no fear, nor shall they grieve."

(al-Baqarah 2: 38)

Allah's Messengers and Prophets brought His guidance and steered mankind to the path of truth and decency. Whereas Satan and his accomplices always tried to tempt them and lead them astray. This battle between good and evil has raged throughout human history. Allah has forbidden all shameful and evil deeds (al-Naḥl 16: 90) and commanded: "Do not even go near to indecencies." (al-An'ām 6: 151); but if we follow Satan then he commands us to engage in such abominable acts.

Al-Faḥshā' is the Qur'ānic term for obscenity and indecency. It means everything that exceeds its limit. However, it is mainly associated with sexual immorality and those acts which human beings instinctively find repulsive. Such vices include adultery, fornication, homosexuality, nudity and pornography or any other obscene act. The wave of modernity that has engulfed us has created a permissive society which has abandoned all moral codes of decency. This has resulted in sexual anarchy. Hence, we witness the uncontrolled indulgence of sexual gratification by unlawful means. Furthermore, the sanctity of marriage no longer exists. Co-habitation has become the prevalent mode of life. There is no shame in indulging in adultery and fornication. There are thousands of teenage pregnancies every year. Even schoolgirls as young as ten or twelve years old are sexually active and many give birth to illegitimate children. To combat this problem the government is providing contraceptive advice in schools and distributing free condoms instead of eradicating the root cause. Brothels are being legalised as the police say they are fighting a losing battle against prostitution. A homosexual relationship is no longer a stigma. Gay and lesbian couples are allowed to marry with legal blessing. The age of sexual acts between consenting people has been lowered to sixteen years. There is no limit on the number of sexual partners one may have. It is not uncommon to see women with four or five children all by different men. No wonder child abuse and incest is rife and that there is an unprecedented increase in sexually transmitted diseases. Pornography has become very big business. It is available through newspapers, magazines, books, films and videos. With the advent of the Internet it has bombarded every household with such ease of access to people of all ages. Sex is used for selling anything from cars, to shoes, to soap powder, to cosmetics and the like. Nudity is widely prevalent and it is very difficult to safeguard one's gaze while walking along the streets or in the parks. By disregarding the commands of Allah we are standing at the edge of a deep abyss. It is the crisis of the standard of right and wrong. By what standard are right and wrong, decent and indecent to be judged? For Muslims the final standard and touchstone is the *Sharīʿah*.

How can we save society and ourselves from this flood of immodesty, shameful and evil deeds? To start with Allah (*swt*) has endowed us with natural modesty, shyness and bashfulness. In Islamic terminology this is called *al-ḥayā'*. In essence, it is a feeling in one's heart that keeps one away from indulging in evil deeds. It is very close to what is termed "one's moral conscience" in Western society. If one has no conscience one can perform and do whatever one likes without a care for what society might think. Conversely, someone with a conscience will feel ashamed to do any evil deed even if no one is watching. The Prophet (*ṣaws*) emphasised this on many occasions.

الْحَيَاءُ وَالإِيْمَانُ قُرِنَا جَمِيْعاً فَإِذَا رُفِعَ أَحَدُهُمَا رُفِعَ الآخَرُ

(الحاكم)

Ḥayā' and *īmān* are two companions that go together. If one of them is lifted, the other is also lifted.

(al-Ḥākim)

It is very obvious from this *ḥadīth* that a person who has no *ḥayā'* lacks faith as well. In another *ḥadīth* the Prophet (*ṣaws*) is reported to have said:

الْحَيَاءُ مِنَ الإِيمَانِ

(مسلم)

Al-ḥayā' is part of *īmān*.

(Muslim)

Thus, *ḥayā'* is the first line of defence against obscenity. It safeguards us from committing indecent acts and our conscience stops us from indulging in vice. As the Prophet (*ṣaws*) observed:

إِنَّ مِمَّا أَدْرَكَ النَّاسُ مِنْ كَلَامِ النُّبُوَّةِ الأُولَى إِذَا لَمْ تَسْتَحْيِ فَافْعَلْ مَا شِئْتَ

(البخاري)

From the words of the previous prophets that the people still find are: "If you feel no shame, then do as you wish."
(Bukhārī)

This means that the importance of and emphasis on modesty has been passed on from earlier prophets. This is the legacy which humanity inherited from time immemorial. It means modesty or shame is the criterion over whether or not one should do something. If one is satisfied that there is no shame in doing something one should do it. But if there is reason to be ashamed when doing such a thing then one should refrain from it.

Other acts forbidden by Allah are evil deeds. In Qur'ānic terminology these are called *munkar*. These refer to actions which human beings abhor. Its opposite is *ma'rūf*. These acts are universally recognised and admired by human beings. The duty assigned to Muslims is called "*Amr bi'l m'arūf wa'l-nahy 'ani'l-munkar*" (to enjoin what is right and forbid what is evil). Evil acts include abusing others, lying, stealing, gambling, giving false evidence, corruption, taking bribes and being dishonest. So our task is both to refrain from committing bad deeds and actively stopping others from committing them. This safeguards society from going astray. This is well illustrated by the story of the people from Banī Isrā'īl who used to live near the sea. As a part of observing the sanctity of the Sabbath they were not allowed to fish on Saturday. Some of them seeing lots of fish on the surface of the water disregarded Allah's command and continued to catch fish on Saturdays. Some concerned people actively remonstrated with them to stop fishing while others who were equally opposed to their transgression said:

وَإِذْ قَالَتْ أُمَّةٌ مِّنْهُمْ لِمَ تَعِظُونَ قَوْمًا ۙ اللَّهُ مُهْلِكُهُمْ أَوْ مُعَذِّبُهُمْ عَذَابًا شَدِيدًا ۖ قَالُوا مَعْذِرَةً إِلَىٰ رَبِّكُمْ وَلَعَلَّهُمْ يَتَّقُونَ ﴿١٦٤﴾

Why do you preach to a people whom Allah will destroy or visit with a terrible punishment? Said the preachers: "To discharge our duty to your Lord and perchance they may fear."

(al-A'rāf 7: 164)

But when Allah's judgement came, those who disobeyed were punished and those who forbade evil were rescued. The fate of those who did not attempt to stop the transgression however is not mentioned. Presumably they perished with the transgressors.

It is our duty to stand up firmly against all evil deeds that are prevalent in society. We may be doing good deeds ourselves and we may, in our hearts, abhor some activities in which society is engaged. But if we do not actively stop others from committing evil deeds we will incur Allah's wrath.

Let us pray that Allah (*swt*) will give us courage to stand firm in our *dīn* and actively preach goodness and stop those who are engaged in wrecking our society with their evil deeds.

(*Āmīn*)

Safeguarding Our Gaze

يَعْلَمُ خَآئِنَةَ ٱلْأَعْيُنِ وَمَا تُخْفِى ٱلصُّدُورُ ﴿١٩﴾

(Allah) knows the treachery of the eyes and all that the hearts conceal.

(Ghāfir 40: 19)

The summer season in Britain comes as a welcome relief after the short and dark days of winter and usually a cold and wet spring. Though pleasant and refreshing this weather usually also brings its own hazards. Many people suffer from hay fever that makes their lives miserable. For students hot days are also associated with the approaching summer examinations that test the efforts and preparation of the whole year. But still the greater test for Muslims, young and old, is how to safeguard their morality and their gaze from straying among the sea of immodesty. Some in the West unashamedly discard their clothes, their bashfulness and modesty, and roam about in near nudity. The scenes of vulgar embraces and petting in parks and shopping centres make one feel very depressed. Yet we also have to be on our guard so that we are not led astray by such obscenity.

Allah (*swt*) has made fornication, adultery and homosexuality unlawful. In order to protect our chastity the *Sharīʿah* has also plugged all those routes through which people slip into wrong deeds. The most important injunction is the "lowering of one's gaze". Allah instructs us in the Holy Qur'ān:

قُل لِّلْمُؤْمِنِينَ يَغُضُّوا۟ مِنْ أَبْصَٰرِهِمْ وَيَحْفَظُوا۟ فُرُوجَهُمْ ۚ ذَٰلِكَ أَزْكَىٰ لَهُمْ ۗ إِنَّ ٱللَّهَ خَبِيرٌۢ بِمَا يَصْنَعُونَ ﴿٣٠﴾

Say to the believing men that they should lower their gaze and guard their modesty: that will make for greater purity for them and Allah is well acquainted with all that they do.
(al-Nūr 24: 30)

This is such an important command that the following verse of *Sūrah al-Nūr* addresses women in a similar manner. Looking at someone whether male or female with lust is unlawful. It is impossible not to see what is happening around you when you walk along the street. Yet try to look away, ignore, and pass by quickly rather than lingering on and continuing to look back at shameful acts. A first look is pardonable but to derive some pleasure by looking again is sinful and we must avoid it. With so much nudity and pornography around us it is very difficult to protect our gaze. As sexually explicit scenes are portrayed in newspapers, magazines, films, television shows and on Internet sites one should consciously make an effort to avoid seeing such material. These provide us with great temptation and we think there is no harm in just having a casual look.

Some people say what harm is there in someone looking at such things in the privacy of his own home. Others think it is only a very slight lapse to look at someone beautiful. It is the same as looking at beautiful flowers, paintings or sculptures. They also argue that they are adult enough not to go astray. Both these views are fallacious. These are the tricks played upon us by Satan. Looking at beautiful flowers or paintings does not incite sexual or lustful feelings. All the research suggests that pornography corrupts. Hence why governments even in the West have enacted laws making the storing of photographic images of children unlawful so as to curb the paedophile menace.

To emphasise the gravity of this sin the Prophet (*ṣaws*) compared it to adultery.

فَزِنَا الْعَيْنِ النَّظَرُ وَزِنَا اللِّسَـــانِ الْمَنْطِقُ وَالنَّفْـــسُ تَمَنَّى وَتَشْتَهِي
وَالْفَرْجُ يُصَدِّقُ ذَلِكَ كُلَّهُ وَيُكَذِّبُهُ

(البخاري ومسلم)

> Eyes commit adultery when they see unlawful things; ears commit adultery when they listen to things unlawful; the tongue commits adultery when it speaks lustful talk and hands commit adultery when they touch and hold prohibited things. The private parts only confirm or refute this [our lust].
>
> (Bukhārī and Muslim)

The same message was given by the Prophet ʿĪsā (peace be upon him). He said:

> You have heard that it was said, 'Do not commit adultery.' But now I tell you: anyone who looks at a woman and wants to possess her is guilty of committing adultery with her in his heart. So if your right eye causes you to sin, take it out and throw it away! It is much better for you to lose part of your body than to have your whole body thrown into hell. If your right hand causes you to sin, then cut it off and throw it away! It is much better for you to lose one of your limbs than for your whole body to go to hell.
>
> (Matthew 5: 27-30)

This is the sin that is very difficult to avoid. Even pious people can be hooked on committing this sin without realising its gravity. When committing other sins people are usually cautious in case others come to know about it. But this sin can be indulged in secretly and no one can tell with what intention you are looking at someone. Committing adultery is difficult, but looking at someone is very easy. Hence this disease destroys the multitudes like an epidemic.

The other problem with lustful gazing is that one never feels satisfied. We can satisfy our hunger and thirst by eating and drinking but we are not satisfied by just looking once or twice. There is a craving for further peeping. Thus, the growing market for pornography. It is even worse if we get into the habit of creating salacious mental images even when we are not looking at something. This indirect pleasure seeking is more fatal as the habit cannot be got rid of.

The verse I have recited at the start of this *khuṭbah* specifies two sins. One is the visual treachery of looking lustfully at prohibited things.

The other is committed by having bad intentions. The verse also informs us that Allah knows about both these sins hidden in our hearts. The implication of His knowing is that He can punish us for our misdeeds. By implication then, if we know that someone is watching over us we will resist temptation. Just as the speed monitoring cameras deter motorists from speeding. Furthermore if we know that there is punishment for our sins then we will try to avoid committing them. Thus both groups of sinners are addressed in this verse.

Having seen the gravity of this sin we should make strenuous efforts to avoid it. To protect us against immorality Allah (*swt*) has imbibed in all human beings a sense of *ḥayā'*. This is an Islamic term that can be translated as shame, bashfulness and modesty. When Adam and Ḥawwā' (peace be upon them) disobeyed Allah, they lost their heavenly attire and became naked. Their impulsive action was to cover themselves with leaves. Thus, *ḥayā'* is our natural defence against immorality. The Prophet (*ṣaws*) said:

إِنَّ مِمَّا أَدْرَكَ النَّاسُ مِنْ كَلَامِ النُّبُوَّةِ الأُولَى إِذَا لَمْ تَسْتَحْيِ فَافْعَلْ مَا شِئْتَ

(البخاري)

From the words of the previous prophets that the people still find are: If you feel no shame, then do as you wish.

(Bukhārī)

If someone's moral conscience is blunted and dead he will feel no shame in doing anything. Hence we should keep our sense of modesty alive and alert so that before doing anything we know that there is no reason to be ashamed of it in front of Allah or the others. The importance of *ḥayā'* is such that it is said by the Prophet that:

الْحَيَاءُ مِنَ الإِيمَانِ

(مسلم)

Al-ḥayā' is a branch of *īmān*.

(Muslim)

Mawlānā Ashraf ʿAlī Thānawī (d.1943), an eminent scholar of Islam, identified three stages for curing this disease. The following represents a summary of his remedies:

> The first, is to resist temptations of the heart. The second is to weaken this urge and desire and then finally kill it altogether. A resisting heart is one trying to avoid its inclination. This is within all our powers. If we involuntarily remember someone then we should try to resist its impact. If your hearts are attracted towards someone beautiful, we should try to think of some ugly and repulsive faces. This will fade the effect on our hearts. This should be further reinforced by thinking that this person will die one day and his/her beautiful body will rot and be eaten by insects. This will weaken the urge. *Dhikr* of Allah and accountability on the Day of Judgement will act as final deterrents. But we should not be impatient as this disease may take a long time to cure. We have to constantly struggle against ourselves to take control over our desires.

In addition to this excellent advice we should always seek Allah's help in protecting us from our carnal desires. Two specific prayers are recorded in the *aḥādīth* which are very effective in controlling lustful gazing and purification of our hearts. These are as follows:

اَللّٰهُمَّ طَهِّرْ قَلْبِي مِنَ النِّفَاقِ وَعَمَلِي مِنَ الرِّيَاءِ ولِسَانِي مِنَ الْكَذِبِ وَعَيْنِي
مِنَ الْخِيَانَةِ فَإِنَّكَ تَعْلَمُ خَائِنَةَ الْأَعْيُنِ وَمَاتُخْفِي الصُّدُوْرُ

(الترمذي)

O my Lord! Purify my heart from hypocrisy and my deeds
from showing-off and my tongue from lying and my
eyes from treachery as You know the treachery of
eyes and what hearts conceal.

(Tirmidhī)

اللَّهُمَّ إِنِّي أَعُوذُ بِكَ مِنْ شَرِّ سَمْعِي وَمِنْ شَرِّ بَصَرِي وَمِنْ شَرِّ لِسَانِي
وَمِنْ شَرِّ قَلْبِي وَمِنْ شَرِّ مَنِيِّي

(أبو داود والترمذي)

O my Lord! I seek Your refuge from the mischief of my ears and the mischief of my eyes and the mischief of my tongue and the mischief of my heart and the mischief of my sexual desires.

(Abū Dā'ūd, Tirmidhī)

Let us pray to Allah (*swt*) that He in His Gracious Mercy saves us from the tricks of Satan, the cursed one, and the mischief of our carnal desires.

(*Āmīn*)

Homosexuality

وَلُوطًا إِذْ قَالَ لِقَوْمِهِۦٓ أَتَأْتُونَ ٱلْفَـٰحِشَةَ مَا سَبَقَكُم بِهَا مِنْ أَحَدٍ مِّنَ
ٱلْعَـٰلَمِينَ ﴿٨٠﴾ إِنَّكُمْ لَتَأْتُونَ ٱلرِّجَالَ شَهْوَةً مِّن دُونِ ٱلنِّسَآءِ ۚ
بَلْ أَنتُمْ قَوْمٌ مُّسْرِفُونَ ﴿٨١﴾

We sent Lūṭ, who said to his people: "Do you commit indecency such as no people in creation (ever) committed before you? Verily you go lustfully to men instead of women! You are indeed a people transgressing beyond bounds."
(al-Aʿrāf 7: 80-81)

It is a catastrophe of modern times that we have lost our firm adherence to many moral norms and values. Hence we are now heading along the slippery road of immorality and decadence. One such indecent act acquiring legal and social approval is homosexuality. During the last 30 years or so this unwholesome way of life has gained momentum and is now prevalent in the Western world without any shame or stigma being attached to it. The age of consent for such indecent activities is gradually being lowered to sixteen years under pressure from the powerful "gay lobby"; this style of life euphemistically being called gay so as to make it attractive and respectable. Homosexuality now enjoys greater acceptance as an alternative lifestyle in the West and it not only affects adults but also even children are lured into experimenting with it. In schools under the rubric of sex education children are taught to respect and tolerate it. There is no discussion about the moral guidance and sinfulness of such acts, which all religions teach.

Unfortunately other religions besides Islam gave way under the pressure of the gay lobby. Their opposition was muted and somehow they gave tacit approval to the Gay Christian Movement and Gay Jews. As there are Gay Blacks and the Gay Asian groups it is inevitable that there will be a Gay Muslims group as well. The formation of a Gay Muslim discussion group on the Internet was founded a few years back. They even publicly participate in Gay Pride celebrations. We are reminded in this respect of the Prophet's (*ṣaws*) prediction that we will follow the People of the Book in all affairs.

Our gut reaction is to condemn the behaviour and practices of these people. But this does not help solve the problem we are facing. Allah (*swt*) sent a special Messenger (Lūṭ) to a people who were indulging in such shameful activities. It is a *fitnah* (trial) and the Muslim society has to deal with it. So what should we do?

We have to firmly declare that this is unlawful activity. This is despite the fact that we will have to face the criticism and endure the wrath of others who openly call Islam backward, homophobic and barbaric. The reality is that human conscience disapproves of bad and evil deeds. To overcome any inner conflict when people want to commit any wrongful act is to give it beautiful names so as to make it palatable. Thus, illegitimate children are called children of "one parent families". Lying is called being economical with the truth. Homosexuals are called gay. All this so that it can justify that there is nothing wrong in being gay and happy. Scientists have now discovered a Gay Gene so as to convince those who want to indulge in this activity that it is quite natural. There is no shame attached to it as they are naturally born with this tendency. Whereas Allah (*swt*) declares:

لَقَدْ خَلَقْنَا ٱلْإِنسَٰنَ فِىٓ أَحْسَنِ تَقْوِيمٍ ﴿٤﴾

We have indeed created human beings in the best of moulds.
(al-Tīn 95: 4)

We should be aware of the fact that Allah has created pairs of male and female in all of creation. It is not only Islam that has outlawed homosexuality but all religions. The punishment of the people of Lūṭ by Allah when they refused to accept his advice was also recorded in the

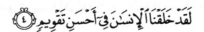

Old Testament (Genesis, Chapter 19) as well as in the Holy Qur'ān. Leviticus, Chapter 20 also legislates against homosexuality.

> If a man has sexual relations with another man, they have done a disgusting thing and both shall be put to death.
>
> (Leviticus 20: 13)

In the New Testament there are generally thought to be three references to homosexuality, all of them in the Pauline Epistles. In two cases passing references are made to homosexual sin within a list of other sins (1 Corinthians 6: 9-10 and 1 Timothy 1: 9-10). It is in the Epistle to the Romans however that the main reference occurs:

> Because they do this, God has given them over to shameful passions. Even the women pervert the natural use of their sex by unnatural acts. In the same way the men gave up natural sexual relations with women and burn their passion for each other. Men do shameful things with each other, as a result they bring upon themselves the punishment they deserve for their wrongdoing.
>
> (Romans 1: 26-27)

Homosexuality, like other matters pertaining to sexuality, is also discussed in the Holy Qur'ān and *aḥādīth* and strictures on such acts are the same as in the Jewish and Christian Scriptures. The following verse in *Sūrah al-Nisā'* deals with this issue:

وَٱلَّذَانِ يَأْتِيَـٰنِهَا مِنكُمْ فَـَٔاذُوهُمَا ۖ فَإِن تَابَا وَأَصْلَحَا
فَأَعْرِضُوا۟ عَنْهُمَآ ۗ إِنَّ ٱللَّهَ كَانَ تَوَّابًا رَّحِيمًا ﴿١٦﴾

If two men among you are guilty of lewdness, punish them both. If they repent and amend, leave them alone; for Allah is Oft-Returning, Most Merciful.

(al-Nisā' 4: 16)

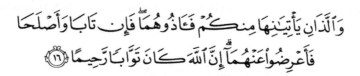

We have to bring these teachings of all religions into the open and not behave like the Christian Church which has almost accepted homosexuality. Now not only are there gay Christians but also gay priests and bishops as well.

To just say that this activity is *ḥarām* (illegal), does not satisfy many young people, as they are used to questioning, discussions and debate. We have to emphasise that we believe that Allah is our Creator, Who created us out of nothing. He is All-Knowing and He knows our nature and our requirements better than we do. He sees everything and guides everyone and He is Most Merciful and Kind. The fact that He has created Adam and his spouse Ḥawwā' (peace be upon them) indicates that the human sexual need is fulfilled by a pair of male and female. This is also manifested in all other creations from the vegetable to the animal kingdom. There is always a pair of male and female in flowers, birds, fishes and animals. This is the natural law of this universe.

One of the aims of sexual relations is the continuity of the human race. Thus, any activity that undermines this natural function destroys society. Hence why homosexuality is termed an unnatural act.

We may well ask then why certain people have homosexual tendencies? Why is it that they feel attracted towards people of their own sex? There is no simple answer. There are however a few factors that we should consider. First, young people are exposed to powerful media displays of sexuality. This puts the wrong ideas in their minds. They are encouraged to explore their sexuality and preferences. Amongst all this a gay life style is presented as an acceptable alternative. Second, it is true that homosexuality is to be found in some societies (including some Muslim societies) where young men are deprived of marriageable females. However this is not the case in the West. Third, there is always a temptation to experiment with things that are forbidden. This is the weapon that Satan, our archenemy, uses in order to destroy us. This is how Adam and Ḥawwā' (peace be upon them) were misled by Satan. In this world we have to endure many tests. When we try to live our lives following the guidance received from Allah, Satan tries to exploit our weaknesses. Some are tempted by Satan to commit wrong deeds to enrich themselves, others are allured by beautiful women or men. Thus, a homosexual tendency may be the result of any one of or a combination of these factors.

To protect ourselves from homosexuality we should take some firm action. It is important that we should emphasise the Islamic practice of keeping these desires under control. The way to safeguard ourselves from developing a homosexual tendency or actual involvement is to remember Allah. This means sincerely following Islamic practices, namely daily prayers, fasting, and supplication to Allah. Prayers protect us from indulging in obscenity and fasting is recommended by the Prophet (*ṣaws*) as a means of controlling lust. As pointed out above this may be a test from Allah or temptation prompted by Satan to deviate us from Allah's path. Hence, we should always seek Allah's refuge from Satan by saying: "I seek refuge of Allah from the accursed Satan." And by reciting *Āyah al-Kursī* (2: 255), *Sūrah al-Falaq* and *Sūrah al-Nās* (the last two *sūrahs*). Another positive step is to emphasise the importance of maintaining Islamic rules of modesty, even with the same sex. This also requires that we control our gaze. Many of us watch television programmes full of sexual foreplay, provocation and innuendo. It all looks innocent enough, yet they are harmful and unsafe scenes to watch. They put the wrong ideas into our minds and whip up sexual emotions. Watching such shows is not permissible for Muslims. Instead Muslims are ordered to lower their gaze even when walking along the street. It is essential to adhere to the Islamic code of dress in front of persons of the same sex, which requires that a man should not see another man's body between the navel and knees. It is also unlawful to see the private parts of others in the flesh or in pictures. It is also not allowed for males or females to sleep together naked under one sheet. Eyes and ears are filters through which things reach our hearts. If we want to keep our hearts pure we have to take care of what we do with our other faculties.

For those who are unfortunately involved in homosexual activity, we should deal with them with sympathy and understanding. As Muslims, our responsibility is to convey the message of Allah to mankind. If we were to hate people and scorn them we cannot hope to reform them. It is only with sincere effort that we can make some progress in reaching the hearts of those whom we would like to follow the right path. Of course there is no question of bullying and ridiculing or oppressing them as sometimes happens. As regards punishment for this sin, we are not here to judge people. There is no specific punishment prescribed by the *Sharīʿah*. Indeed jurists have held differing opinions about the punishment for this practice. Such punishment can only be meted out by an Islamic state. The verse from *Sūrah al-Nisā'* quoted above states: "If they repent and amend leave them alone; for Allah is Oft-Returning, Most Merciful" (4: 16). We should also follow the example of the Prophet 'Īsā' (peace be upon him) who pleaded for his *Ummah* and sought forgiveness for them by imploring Allah (*swt*):

إِن تُعَذِّبْهُمْ فَإِنَّهُمْ عِبَادُكَ وَإِن تَغْفِرْ لَهُمْ فَإِنَّكَ أَنتَ ٱلْعَزِيزُ ٱلْحَكِيمُ ﴿١١٨﴾

If You punish them they are Your servants. If You forgive them, You are the Exalted in Power, the Wise.

(al-Mā'idah 5: 118)

Let us pray that Allah enables us to follow the path of Islam and leads us not into temptation as we live in a permissive and lax society.

(*Āmīn*)

Further Reading

- 'Gay, Muslim and Controversial.' *Q News,* December 1999, pp.17-19
- Helena Jeffs: 'Age of Consent' for Male Homosexual Acts. House of Commons Library, 1994 (Research Paper 94/12)
- Simon Le Vay: 'Sex and the Single Gene.' *The Times Higher Supplement,* May 3, 1996

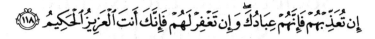

Society and the Islamic Social Order

يَٰٓأَيُّهَا ٱلنَّاسُ إِنَّا خَلَقْنَٰكُم مِّن ذَكَرٍ وَأُنثَىٰ وَجَعَلْنَٰكُمْ شُعُوبًا وَقَبَآئِلَ لِتَعَارَفُوٓا۟ ۚ
إِنَّ أَكْرَمَكُمْ عِندَ ٱللَّهِ أَتْقَىٰكُمْ ۚ إِنَّ ٱللَّهَ عَلِيمٌ خَبِيرٌ ﴿١٣﴾

O mankind! We have created you from a single (pair) of male and female, and made you into nations and tribes, that you may know each other (not that you may despise each other). Verily the most honoured of you in the sight of Allah is (he who is) the most righteous of you. And Allah has full knowledge and is well-acquainted (with all things).

(al-Ḥujurāt 49: 13)

Society, in Islam is an association, formed according to Divine Law, for the purpose of harmonious and peaceful co-existence. It is the scheme of life where the Oneness of God (*Tawḥīd*) is expressed in the Unity of Man. The logical conclusion of this belief is that Islamic society is neither sectarian, nor racial but harmonious and universal. According to Islam, if there is real difference between man and man it cannot be on the basis of race, colour, country of birth or language. It is only beliefs, principles and ideas that distinguish one person from another. On this basis Islam seeks to build a principled and ideological society which is very different from the racial, nationalist and linguistic societies that exist today. The Islamic social order transcends all geographical boundaries and barriers of race, colour and language. Thus, Islamic ideology is appropriate for all parts of the world and for all races as its foundation is the universal brotherhood of mankind. Those who accept its creed and moral standards become part of the Muslim *Ummah*. Those who do not accept its creed do not belong to the *Ummah*, yet they are treated with tolerance and humanity. Their basic human rights are guaranteed. Under Islamic law all these rights are granted by God, hence they cannot be abrogated or changed by any Muslim government.

Islam views society as a divinely ordained institution necessary for man's fulfilment of the purpose of his creation. According to the Islamic teachings man is created as a vicegerent (*Khalīfah*) of God on earth. As narrated in *Sūrah al-Baqarah* (2: 30-34) Allah (*swt*) declared before the angels: "I will create a vicegerent on earth." The angels were surprised and questioned why He would place on earth a creature which is capable of doing evil? God answered that He had indeed a purpose unknown to the angels who cannot but obey God. The purpose behind man's creation consists of fulfilling the moral part of Divine Will a part whose fulfilment requires that the subject be free to fulfil as well as to violate it. Being alone capable of moral action man is indeed God's "Best and the Supreme" creation and is higher than angels.

There are several implications of the story of Adam (peace be upon him) and man's vicegerency (*Khilāfah*): First, although the first human pair disobeyed Allah's command, the narration in the Qur'ān does not subscribe to the view that the woman led the man to sin and disobedience. According to the Qur'ān, "Satan causes them both to deflect". Both were held responsible for the act, both repented for their transgression and both were forgiven. Thus, they entered the world without any stigma of "original sin" on their souls. In this way Islam does not accept the belief of "fall of Adam". Man was created for the purpose of acting as vicegerent on earth and to fulfil his mission. This is an honour bestowed by the Creator and represents the "Rise of Man" to a new assignment.

Second, the role and status of vicegerency is conferred upon the human race. As such man and woman alike share it. This lays the foundation for their essential equality as human beings, as vicegerents of God on earth, whatever different roles they perform in society.

Third, human nature is pure and good. Man is created in the best of forms. Both man and woman are made of the same substance. Everyone is born in a state of purity and innocence. Success and failure depends entirely on one's own belief and behaviour. No one is responsible for the shortcomings of others.

Fourth, man has been given freedom of choice. He is free to accept or deny reality. He is responsible for his acts, but he is not deprived of his freedom, even if he makes mistakes and abuses it. The uniqueness of the human situation lies in man's psychosocial volition. This potential enables him to rise to the highest pinnacle or to fall into the deepest abyss.

Fifth, the dangers of misuse of freedom continue to confront man throughout his life on earth. The challenge from Satan is unceasing. To safeguard man against this Divine Guidance is provided.

Sixth, man has not been totally protected against error. This would have involved negation of freedom of choice. He may commit errors, but his redemption lies in his realisation of those errors, in seeking repentance and turning back to the right path.

Having seen the purpose of human creation, we can understand the importance of society in which human beings flourish. Society is necessary for the acquisition of knowledge. Allah no doubt, endows this knowledge. He taught Adam the necessary knowledge and gave him guidance to live on earth and this knowledge is transmitted through one generation to succeeding generations. This knowledge has progressed by virtue of the mutual consultation, criticism and validation of other human beings. Such a cumulative advance in human knowledge and skills is only possible through society. All knowledge must be tested against the evidence and experience of others. Thus the Islamic concept of *shūrā* (consultation, dialogue and argument) is declared a sound method by the Qur'ān for the governance of human affairs. It is through *ijmā*ʿ (the consensus of the *Ummah*) and *ijtihād* (creativity) that society can progress and solve its problems. Man cannot achieve the Truth except through following these principles.

Again, society is necessary for morality. Our ethical values require the existence of others. It is only through mutual interaction that moral response and ethical action, if required, can be taken. It cannot be practised in a vacuum. It is impossible for love, charity, justice and sacrifice for example to be realised unless there are other humans to be loved, to be charitable to and just to, to assist and rescue through sacrifice.

Finally, society is necessary for history. According to Islam the purpose of creation is the realisation of God's will on this earth. Therefore, history and its processes is the arena for morality – they are imperative – and our involvement in them is to actualise the history and fulfilment of Divine Will. Thus, there is no separation of religion and state in Islam. This is why the Muslims could not allow history to be directed by chance, or by powerful rulers. This is why the Prophet established the Islamic State in Madinah soon after his migration, so that purposes of morality can be realised and enforced.

As mentioned before, the Islamic social order is based on revelation from Allah, the Creator of the Universe. It is based on brotherhood where every member is equal, but "the most honoured of you in the sight of Allah is (he who is) the most righteous of you" (al-Ḥujurāt 49: 13). The cement that bonds Islamic society together is mutual love and affection. The Prophet (*ṣaws*) said that Muslims are like a body: if one part aches the whole body feels the pain. It is a caring society in which the poor and needy are looked after. There is respect for elders and mercy for the young. There is hospitality for guests and strangers. There is compassion for the sick and downtrodden. There is participation in marriages and funerals. There is respect for education and knowledge and there is modesty in all affairs. These in brief are the characteristics of the Islamic society.

Let us pray that Allah may help us to establish a caring and sharing society so that humanity lives on this earth in peace and harmony.

(*Āmīn*)

Further Reading

- Mohammad Muslehuddin: *Sociology and Islam: a Comparative Study of Islam and its Social System*. Lahore: Islamic Publications, 1977
- Ismail R. Faruqi: *Islam and Culture*. Kuala Lumpur: ABIM, 1980

Family Life

يَـٰٓأَيُّهَا ٱلنَّاسُ ٱتَّقُوا۟ رَبَّكُمُ ٱلَّذِى خَلَقَكُم مِّن نَّفْسٍ وَٰحِدَةٍ وَخَلَقَ مِنْهَا زَوْجَهَا وَبَثَّ
مِنْهُمَا رِجَالًا كَثِيرًا وَنِسَآءً ۚ وَٱتَّقُوا۟ ٱللَّهَ ٱلَّذِى تَسَآءَلُونَ بِهِۦ وَٱلْأَرْحَامَ ۚ إِنَّ
ٱللَّهَ كَانَ عَلَيْكُمْ رَقِيبًا ﴿١﴾

O mankind! Fear your Lord, Who created you from a single person, created, of like nature, his mate, from them twain scattered (like seeds) countless men and women; fear Allah, through Whom you demand your mutual rights, and the wombs (that bore you): for Allah ever watches over you.

(al-Nisā' 4: 1)

We are living in a critical age where institutions that were the bedrock of humanity are challenged and the very foundations of contemporary society are endangered by the anarchic waves of unbelief and materialism. The first victim of its onslaught has been the family. The institution of marriage that was once honoured and held in high esteem in all cultures and religions is gradually being replaced by cohabitation. This is nothing less than living together in sin. Furthermore, there is no shame attached to birthing illegitimate children; instead it is euphemistically called the one parent family. The relationship of husband and wife is replaced by one of partnership as if it were some sort of commercial enterprise. Against all these odds, the Muslim family with its ideals and norms of morality and decency has to be the standardbearer of this institution.

According to Islamic teachings, the family is a divinely inspired institution. In the verse I recited at the start of this *khuṭbah* Allah says that He has created us from a single soul and from the first couple the human race multiplied and progressed. There are two further implications arising from this verse. First, Allah is the sole Creator of this world as well as the human race. Second, all of us are equal before our Lord. Differences based on caste, colour, race and language should not divide us and create artificial frictions and disharmony.

In another verse, in *Sūrah al-Rūm* the creation of human beings and marriage ties are described as Allah's Signs on which we are asked to reflect.

وَمِنْ ءَايَٰتِهِۦٓ أَنْ خَلَقَ لَكُم مِّنْ أَنفُسِكُمْ أَزْوَٰجًا لِّتَسْكُنُوٓا۟ إِلَيْهَا وَجَعَلَ
بَيْنَكُم مَّوَدَّةً وَرَحْمَةً ۚ إِنَّ فِى ذَٰلِكَ لَءَايَٰتٍ لِّقَوْمٍ يَتَفَكَّرُونَ ﴿٢١﴾

And among His Signs is this, that He created for you mates from among yourselves, that you may dwell in tranquillity with them, and He has put love and mercy between your (hearts): verily in that are Signs for those who reflect.
(al-Rūm 30: 21)

Sexual attraction between males and females is natural. This is regulated by the institution of marriage that is bonded by love and affection. The couple has to bear sacrifices to bring up their children and thus help perpetuate the human race.

To keep the marriage ties firm the couple solemnly enter into a binding contract. In Islamic terminology marriage is called *'aqd* meaning a knot or a contract. In *Sūrah al-Nisā'* (4: 21) this is referred to as *mīthāqan ghalīẓā* (a strong covenant). Thus in Islam marriage is a social contract but it is also a sacred contract. Faith constitutes the firm foundation for the institution of marriage. As this relationship is close an intimate sharing of faith is essential. Thus Muslims are not allowed to marry people of other faiths. The only exception is that a Muslim man can marry Jewish or Christian women as their religions are based on revealed books. A Muslim woman however is not permitted to marry a Jewish or Christian man or anyone who is not a Muslim. Thus, faith plays an important role in family relations. If one spouse changes his or her faith the marriage has to be dissolved. Similarly a son cannot inherit from his father if he changes his faith.

The family plays a vital role in Muslim society. This importance is manifested by the fact that one-third of legal injunctions in the Holy Qur'ān relate to family matters. The other distinguishing feature of a Muslim family is that unlike its Western counterpart it is not nuclear in nature but is rather an extended family system. This plays an important role in the socialisation and transfer of values from one generation to the next. It helps children to grow among a wider circle of relatives and helps parents as well in sharing the burden of child rearing and parenting. At the same time it provides a valuable safety net providing social and economic support to members of the extended family. Furthermore, the Islamic law of inheritance recognises the rights of relatives and wealth is distributed among them. This prevents the concentration of wealth in a few hands as it is dispersed among the wider circle.

In an Islamic marriage both partners are bound together yet their roles and responsibilities are different. This reflects the differences in their physical and psychological make-up. As men are physically stronger and capable of hard work they are required to be the breadwinner for the family. Women as they have to bear children and devote their energies to looking after them are required to concentrate on the home. In this way both husband and wife help each other in bringing up the children and are responsible for their education and training. This division of labour is equitable and creates stability in the home and in society.

Above all the family provides the psychological and emotional stability for the couple. In the verse quoted above from *Sūrah al-Rūm* Allah points out that spouses find consolation, rest and tranquillity in their relationship. In *Sūrah al-Baqarah* a metaphor of dress is used to describe the intimate relationship between husband and wife. Allah says: "They are a garment for you and you are a garment for them." (2: 187) Prof. Khurshid Ahmad explaining this verse in his book *Family Life in Islam* writes:

> This emphasises their sameness, their oneness, something much more sublime than legal equality. The husband and wife both are described as each other's raiment, not one as the garment and the other the body. A garment is something nearest to the human body; it is that part of the external world, which becomes a part of our being. Such is the closeness of the relationship between the spouses.

> Dress is something that covers the body and protects it. The spouses are protectors and guardians of each other. The dress beautifies the wearer. One feels oneself incomplete without it. Husband and wife complement each other; one completes and perfects and beautifies the other. This relationship also protects morals – without this shield one is exposed to the dangers of illicit carnality. (p.21)

It is worth noting that sexual relations outside marriage are considered a criminal act and are punishable under Islamic law. Family life by contrast provides companionship, love and affection that give peace of mind. Hence why the Prophet (*ṣaws*) said that home is the best place in the world.

However, despite this very close and loving relationship between spouses, disputes and friction can sometimes occur. Such is human nature. Islam tries to solve this problem by providing a system of reconciliation through impartial arbitrators from the two families. Their efforts help to solve the problem within both families. Sometimes even this may not succeed and then the only solution is dissolution of the marriage. Unlike a Christian marriage *ʿaqd* is not a sacrament which is irreversible. There is provision for the divorce and re-marriage of both spouses.

We have made our homes in this country hence it is our duty to follow and practise Islamic values and try to introduce them to our hosts. Western society has abandoned its own old values, which has led to the disintegration of family life and an undermining of the institution of marriage. Let our neighbours observe the peaceful and harmonious family of our homes. This will be the practical demonstration of how society can live in peace and tranquillity.

Let us pray that Allah may guide us to follow His Commands in our family life and help us to create a blissful society.

(*Āmīn*)

Kindness to Parents and Relations

وَٱعْبُدُوا۟ ٱللَّهَ وَلَا تُشْرِكُوا۟ بِهِۦ شَيْـًٔا ۖ وَبِٱلْوَٰلِدَيْنِ إِحْسَٰنًا وَبِذِى
ٱلْقُرْبَىٰ وَٱلْيَتَٰمَىٰ وَٱلْمَسَٰكِينِ وَٱلْجَارِ ذِى ٱلْقُرْبَىٰ وَٱلْجَارِ
ٱلْجُنُبِ وَٱلصَّاحِبِ بِٱلْجَنۢبِ وَٱبْنِ ٱلسَّبِيلِ وَمَا مَلَكَتْ
أَيْمَٰنُكُمْ ۗ إِنَّ ٱللَّهَ لَا يُحِبُّ مَن كَانَ مُخْتَالًا فَخُورًا ﴿٣٦﴾

Serve Allah, and join not any partners with Him. And do good – to parents, kinsfolk, and orphans, and those who are in need, neighbours who are relations, neighbours who are strangers, the companion by your side, the wayfarer (you meet) and what your right hands possess; for Allah loves not the arrogant, the vainglorious.

(al-Nisā' 4: 36)

Kindness to our parents and relations is the second commandment after worshipping Allah alone. The rights of parents come first, as they are the ones who brought us into this world and it is they who looked after us when we were helpless babies. Their love and unflinching devotion throughout our infancy and later on helped us to educate and train ourselves to live in this world. We owe them so much that we can never repay them.

So what are parents' rights? Of course we love them and should respect them. We should treat them well and honour them. All these acts should be done out of sincerity not just as a token of affection. These acts of kindness, love and respect are explained in *Sūrah al-Isrā'* as follows:

وَقَضَىٰ رَبُّكَ أَلَّا تَعْبُدُوٓاْ إِلَّآ إِيَّاهُ وَبِٱلْوَٰلِدَيْنِ إِحْسَٰنًا ۚ إِمَّا يَبْلُغَنَّ عِندَكَ
ٱلْكِبَرَ أَحَدُهُمَآ أَوْ كِلَاهُمَا فَلَا تَقُل لَّهُمَآ أُفٍّ وَلَا تَنْهَرْهُمَا وَقُل
لَّهُمَا قَوْلًا كَرِيمًا ﴿٢٣﴾ وَٱخْفِضْ لَهُمَا جَنَاحَ ٱلذُّلِّ مِنَ ٱلرَّحْمَةِ
وَقُل رَّبِّ ٱرْحَمْهُمَا كَمَا رَبَّيَانِى صَغِيرًا ﴿٢٤﴾ رَّبُّكُمْ أَعْلَمُ بِمَا فِى نُفُوسِكُمْ ۚ
إِن تَكُونُوا۟ صَٰلِحِينَ فَإِنَّهُۥ كَانَ لِلْأَوَّٰبِينَ غَفُورًا ﴿٢٥﴾

Your Lord has decreed that you worship none but Him and that you be kind to parents. Whether one or both of them attain old age in your life, say not to them a word of contempt, nor repel them, but address them in terms of honour. And out of kindness, lower to them the wing of humility, and say: "My Lord! Bestow on them Your mercy even as they cherished me in childhood." Your Lord knows best what is in your hearts. If you do deeds of righteousness, verily He is Most Forgiving to those who turn to Him again and again.

(al-Isrā' 17: 23-25)

A more difficult demand is their obedience. Yet their disobedience is a major sin. Once the Prophet (*ṣaws*) said to his Companions: "Should I tell you what are major sins?" The Companions replied: "Yes indeed". The Prophet said: "To associate partners with Allah and disobey parents." He was sitting reclining and he straightened his posture and said twice: "To give false evidence" (Tirmidhī). In Islam, obedience of Allah and His Prophet (*ṣaws*) is absolute but obedience of other human beings is conditional. If by obeying other people in authority one would be disobeying Allah and His Prophet's (*ṣaws*) commands then it is permissible to disobey such commands. Furthermore, there is a *ḥadīth* of the Prophet which states:

لَاطَاعَةَ لِمَخْلُوقٍ فِي مَعْصِيَةِ الْخَالِقِ

(البغوي، شرح السنّة)

Obedience of other created beings is not lawful if it leads to disobedience of the Creator.

(*Sharḥ al-Sunnah*)

As it is the mother who bears such a heavy burden in carrying the child, and who suffers agony in childbirth and then spends time nursing the baby, Allah (*swt*) has raised her status by giving her precedence over the father.

جَاءَ رَجُلٌ إِلَى رَسُولِ اللَّهِ صَلَّى اللَّهُ عَلَيْهِ وَسَلَّمَ فَقَالَ يَارَسُولَ اللَّهِ مَنْ أَحَقُّ النَّاسِ بِحُسْنِ صَحَابَتِي؟ قَالَ أُمُّكَ قَالَ ثُمَّ مَنْ؟ قَالَ ثُمَّ أُمُّكَ قَالَ ثُمَّ مَنْ؟ قَالَ ثُمَّ أُمُّكَ قَالَ ثُمَّ مَنْ؟ قَالَ ثُمَّ أَبُوكَ

(البخاري ومسلم)

When someone asked the Prophet (*ṣaws*) who deserved most of his courtesy and good manners, the Prophet replied: "Your mother". He then asked who after that. The Prophet again replied: "Your mother". He repeated the same question and still the Prophet replied: "Your mother". When he asked the same question the fourth time, the Prophet said: "Your father".

(Bukhārī and Muslim)

This illustrates the high rank Islam assigns to mothers. In another *ḥadīth* the Prophet (*ṣaws*) is reported to have said to one of his Companions:

الْزَمْهَا فَإِنَّ الْجَنَّةَ عِنْدَ رِجْلِهَا (أحمد)

"Be close to her for truly Paradise lies at her feet."

(Aḥmad)

To love, respect and obey one's parents is part of the *Sharī'ah* of earlier prophets as well. The Qur'ān mentions this categorically as:

وَإِذْ أَخَذْنَا مِيثَٰقَ بَنِىٓ إِسْرَٰٓءِيلَ لَا تَعْبُدُونَ إِلَّا ٱللَّهَ وَبِٱلْوَٰلِدَيْنِ إِحْسَانًا وَذِى ٱلْقُرْبَىٰ وَٱلْيَتَٰمَىٰ وَٱلْمَسَٰكِينِ وَقُولُوا۟ لِلنَّاسِ حُسْنًا ... ﴿٨٣﴾

And remember We took a Covenant from the Children of Israel (to this effect): Worship none but Allah; treat with kindness your parents and relations and orphans and those in need; speak fair to people...

(al-Baqarah 2: 83)

The real test of obeying this commandment is looking after one's parents in their old age. At that time they are infirm and weak and may be economically not well off. Thus looking after them and serving them ungrudgingly tests the patience of their children. The Islamic teaching is not to abandon them in their homes or dump them in old people's homes or leave them to be cared for by the State's social services department, where they have to spend the remainder of their lives in misery and loneliness. Modern society has provided homes for old people with the pretext of looking after them. But this causes more emotional upheaval. What old people need is not only physical care but also fulfilment of their emotional needs. Islam wants that they should be part of our extended families and that they live with their children and grandchildren. Parents' rights are not only a moral obligation but are instead enforceable by the Islamic State. During the time of 'Umar ibn al-Khaṭṭāb, the second *Khalīfah*, an old person was living alone in poverty. 'Umar inquired about his relations and was told that he had no one except his nephew. 'Umar ordered his nephew to care for his uncle, as he was legally responsible for him. It is sad to see many old people neglected by their children and relations and dependent on state charity.

After our parents other near relations, brothers, sisters, uncles and aunts and grandparents deserve our love, respect and economic help if they are in need. Islam does not favour nuclear families, where husband, wife and offspring cater for their own needs. The Islamic family is an extended family where grandparents, uncles and aunts and other relations either live together or in close proximity. They look after each other. This is how the cultural values of Islamic faith are transmitted from one generation to the next. Parents do not usually have much spare time to spend with their children. Thus, they are brought up under the supervision of grandparents who need the company of the young in their retirement. Children are brought up in a group of close relations and they develop love and an understanding of social life. In this way, there are fewer causes of family breakdown resulting in broken homes and neglect of children. Even if both parents are working there are other members of the family to look after them. There is less likelihood of child abuse by parents if there are others around to watch what is happening.

The extended family also provides support during times of illness and infirmity. All members of the family join in to provide help and solace to those who are in need. This help and support is also available to those members of the family who are disabled, unemployed or poor. Instead of looking to the state for means-tested help the family provides a cushion to overcome all problems within its environment. This is a more dignified and self-respecting solution to such problems.

Our society spends huge amounts of resources, both human and capital, in keeping our neighbourhoods safe and crime free. The most petty crimes and vandalism are caused by juvenile delinquents as they are called. These young hooligans and criminals are the result of broken homes. They have nowhere to spend their time. There is no one to supervise them and spend time with them to provide love, care and support. Inevitably, they develop anti-social behaviour and embark upon a career of vandalism. They are involved in drug taking and to finance their habit resort to stealing. When they are bored they embark on destruction and wreckage. Islam strengthens family life and binds people together. It creates a caring family that leads to a caring society.

Let us pray that we remain observant of our duties to our parents and relations. That we treat them with love, respect and honour. That we help in creating a caring society.

(Āmīn)

The Rights of Children

إِنَّمَآ أَمْوَٰلُكُمْ وَأَوْلَٰدُكُمْ فِتْنَةٌ ۚ وَٱللَّهُ عِندَهُۥٓ أَجْرٌ عَظِيمٌ ﴿١٥﴾

Your riches and your children are but a trial, and with Allah is the highest reward.

(al-Taghābun 64: 15)

It is observed that in our society there is a great deal of emphasis on the rights of parents and elders. It is expected that they should be treated with respect and honour. Of course this is how it should be. Our parents and elders deserve to be honoured and respected. But at the same time we should not neglect the rights of children and the young. The Prophet (*ṣaws*) said:

لَيْسَ مِنَّا مَنْ لَمْ يَرْحَمْ صَغِيرَنَا وَلَمْ يُوَقِّرْ كَبِيرَنَا (الترمذي)

The one who is not kind to our youngsters and who does not respect our elders is not one of us.

(Tirmidhī)

In this *ḥadīth* the Prophet enunciated the basic principles on which our society should operate. Love, kindness and affection for the young and respect and regard for elders.

If we look at the human life cycle it is the child whose rights precede. It is the child who requires all the care and attention as well as the love and affection to grow up. Only later on can he reciprocate the tender care, which his parents showered on him. Only then in the words of the

Qur'ān can he pray: "My Lord! Bestow on them Your mercy as they cherished me in childhood" (al-Isrā' 17: 24).

So what are the rights of children? To start with a child is accorded legal status while he is still a foetus in his mother's womb. Thus, the foetus should not be deliberately aborted. This is tantamount to murder. Unfortunately in our society thousands of abortions are carried out without any guilt of murder. It is argued that it is the woman's right to decide whether to bear children or seek an abortion. According to Islamic teachings, however, everything we possess including our lives belong to Allah. Thus, it is illegal to commit suicide, as we have no right to take our lives. In earlier times people used to kill infants as they seemed to be a burden on them and an economic liability. However we forget that it is the Creator Who is the real Provider and Sustainer. There is a specific prohibition on infanticide in the Qur'ān as females were the main target of this crime. The pagan Arabs considered girls as a disgrace. This crime against children's lives is characterised as one of the great sins.

وَلَا تَقْتُلُوٓا أَوْلَٰدَكُمْ خَشْيَةَ إِمْلَٰقٍ نَّحْنُ نَرْزُقُهُمْ وَإِيَّاكُمْ إِنَّ قَتْلَهُمْ
كَانَ خِطْـًٔا كَبِيرًا ﴿٣١﴾

Kill not your children for fear of want: We shall provide sustenance for them as well as you. Verily the killing of them is a great sin.

(al-Isrā' 17: 31)

After the birth of a child the first duty of parents is to say *adhān* and *iqāmah* in their ears. Thus, the child listens to Allah's name soon after birth. Incidentally there is no *adhān* and *iqāmah* said before funeral prayers as these are already said at the time of birth. As we know, the prayers start just after *iqāmah*, and symbolically show that life indeed is very short. It is also the duty of parents to give children good names so that later on they are not embarrassed by something inappropriate. In this respect, the name should not mean something bad or undesirable. Hence why the Prophet changed the names of several Companions, as they were considered inappropriate.

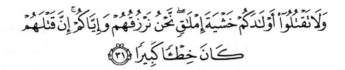

The home is the child's first school. It is at home where he learns to speak and acquire habits. It is the parents' duty to rear their children in such a way that they become good members of society. They should be taught basic Islamic knowledge and duties. In *Sūrah Ṭā Hā* the Prophet (*ṣaws*) is asked to: "Enjoin Prayers on your family, and be constant therein" (20: 132). The best gifts that parents can give to their children are good manners and a decent education. There are several *aḥādīth* alluding to this: Sa'īd ibn al-'Āṣ relates that the Prophet (*ṣaws*) said:

مَا نَحَلَ وَالِدٌ وَلَدًا مِنْ نَحْلٍ أَفْضَلَ مِنْ أَدَبٍ حَسَنٍ (الترمذي)

A father cannot give a better gift to his son
than good manners.

(Tirmidhī)

It is reported by Anas that the Prophet (*ṣaws*) said:

أَكْرِمُوا أَوْلَادَكُمْ وَأَحْسِنُوا أَدَبَهُمْ (ابن ماجة)

Respect your children and adorn them with
the best manners.

(Ibn Mājah)

Children learn their habits and attitudes by observing their parents and other close relations. If parents are not a very good role model any amount of advice and exhortation will be ineffective. The reason behind this is very simple: a person is not impressed by what he hears but by what he observes. When children see that their parents are not doing what they are asking them to do then all their words of wisdom will be fruitless.

It is related about a learned person that once a mother brought her son to him and asked him to advise her son not to eat too much sweet stuffs. The learned man asked her to bring the boy back the following week. When she did, he told the child: "Do not eat excessive sweet stuffs." The mother was surprised and asked that if this was the only piece of advice he had to offer why he hadn't said the same on their first visit. The learned man replied that last week he was indulging himself in eating sweet stuffs. Hence it was not right for him to advise against this habit. Now he had abstained from sweets for the whole week and could give this advice to others.

Children by nature are inquisitive. They acquire knowledge by asking questions about everything they do not understand. Sometimes their questions may sound awkward, yet it is the duty of parents to treat all questions seriously and to try to provide appropriate answers. They should train their children especially when they are grown up to discuss issues and argue properly. It is ill advised to shut them up if parents do not know the answer or are unable to satisfy them. A frank admission of ignorance is much appreciated by children rather than just saying what they believe in and that something does not require further discussion.

The parents of teenagers need different skills to cope with them. Small children need more care and protection and at times some authoritarian discipline. But when children have grown up they then need more freedom and want to make their own choices in clothes and the like. This may conflict with the preferences of their parents. All such issues should be tackled with tact and good humour. Convincing them intellectually is more effective than prescribing edicts.

Children need love and care from their parents. Of course Allah has created this love in the hearts of parents. We observe this in animals and birds: how lovingly they look after their young ones. Yet this love has to be demonstrated by a loving and caring attitude. Once Aqraʿ ibn Ḥābis, a Companion, saw the Prophet (*ṣaws*) kissing Ḥasan, one of his grandsons. He commented in amazement: "I have ten sons and I never kissed one of them ever." The Prophet (*ṣaws*) replied:

مَنْ لَا يَرْحَمُ النَّاسَ لَا يَرْحَمُهُ اللهُ عَزَّ وَجَلَّ (مسلم)

> The one who does not show mercy cannot have mercy shown to him by Allah, the Mighty and the Majestic.
>
> (Muslim)

In another *ḥadīth* by *Umm al-Mu'minīn* 'Ā'ishah, she narrates that some villagers came to meet the Prophet (*ṣaws*) and asked him about whether he kissed his children to which the Prophet replied "Yes". They said: "By God we never kiss our children." To this the Prophet replied:

أَوَ أَمْلِكُ لَكَ أَنْ نَزَعَ اللَّهُ مِنْ قَلْبِكَ الرَّحْمَةَ (مسلم)

If Allah has taken away mercy from your hearts
what can I do.

(Muslim)

The other important facet of family life is justice. It is the right of children that parents treat all their offspring justly. If one child gets more favourable treatment from his parents it makes his brothers or sisters jealous. This can lead to rejection and depression. Sometimes boys receive preferential treatment over girls. Unfortunately in some families girls are still considered inferior despite the very clear injunctions of Allah and His Messenger. Nauʿmān ibn Bashīr narrates that the Prophet (*ṣaws*) said:

اعْدِلُوا بَيْنَ أَوْلَادِكُمْ (النسائي)

O People! Do justice among your children.

(Nasā'ī)

He also narrates an incident about his father, who gave him some wealth as a gift. His mother said that I would not agree about this gift until I take guidance from Allah's Prophet. When his father went to the Prophet and told him about this gift, the Prophet asked him "Have you given a similar gift to your other children?" He replied: "No, I have not." The Prophet said:

اِتَّقُوا اللَّهَ وَاعْدِلُوا بَيْنَ أَوْلَادِكُمْ (النسائي)

Fear Allah and do justice among your children.

(Nasā'ī)

His father returned and rescinded the gift.

Muslim parents living in the West inevitably face enormous problems with their children. When children are being educated in Western schools alongside children of other faiths or no faith, they face tremendous peer pressure to conform to the majority mode of behaviour. They are also subjected to a media onslaught that erodes Islamic values. It is the duty of parents to oversee their children's friends and monitor what TV programmes they watch. Mere exhortations and enforced obedience of Islamic values will not have a lasting effect. Unless children can be convinced of the authenticity of their faith and have a firm conviction to follow it, superficial adherence may last for a few years only and later on they will abandon it or rebel altogether.

Parenting is a difficult and arduous task, yet it is also fulfilling and rewarding. We should pray to Allah that He may enable us to accomplish this trial with success and be able to say in the Hereafter:

قَالُوٓاْ إِنَّا كُنَّا قَبۡلُ فِيٓ أَهۡلِنَا مُشۡفِقِينَ ﴿٢٦﴾ فَمَنَّ ٱللَّهُ عَلَيۡنَا وَوَقَىٰنَا عَذَابَ
ٱلسَّمُومِ ﴿٢٧﴾ إِنَّا كُنَّا مِن قَبۡلُ نَدۡعُوهُۖ إِنَّهُۥ هُوَ ٱلۡبَرُّ ٱلرَّحِيمُ ﴿٢٨﴾

We were aforetime in the midst of our household, ever in dread. Therefore Allah obliged us, and has protected us from the torment of the Scorching Wind. We used to pray to Him aforetime. Verily it is He, the Beneficent, the Merciful.

(al-Ṭūr 52: 26-28)

Further Reading

— Ruqaiyyah Waris Maqsood: *Living with Teenagers: a Guide for Muslim Parents*. London: TaHa Publishers, 1995

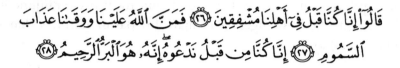

Our Own Rights

وَلَقَدْ كَرَّمْنَا بَنِيٓ ءَادَمَ وَحَمَلْنَٰهُمْ فِي ٱلْبَرِّ وَٱلْبَحْرِ وَرَزَقْنَٰهُم مِّنَ ٱلطَّيِّبَٰتِ
وَفَضَّلْنَٰهُمْ عَلَىٰ كَثِيرٍ مِّمَّنْ خَلَقْنَا تَفْضِيلًا ﴿٧٠﴾

We have honoured the progeny of Adam; provided them with transport on land and sea; given them sustenance: things good and pure; and conferred on them special favours above a great part of Our creation.

(al-Isrā' 17: 70)

Human beings by nature tend to be selfish. They are keen to protect their self-interest and to achieve their desire they sometimes even trample upon the rights of others. Yet at times in an excessive zeal for piety some people leave the path of moderation and adopt a life of self-denial and self-torment. Both these attitudes are wrong. We are required to respect the rights of others but at the same time we should also respect our own rights. This is well illustrated by the advice given by the Prophet (*ṣaws*) to some of his Companions who were anxious to practise celibacy, constant night vigil and fasting in order to achieve nearness to Allah (*swt*). The Prophet (*ṣaws*) warned them, saying:

أَمَا وَاللَّهِ إِنِّي لَأَخْشَاكُمْ لِلَّهِ وَأَتْقَاكُمْ لَهُ لَكِنِّي أَصُومُ وَأُفْطِرُ وَأُصَلِّي
وَأَرْقُدُ وَأَتَزَوَّجُ النِّسَاءَ فَمَنْ رَغِبَ عَنْ سُنَّتِي فَلَيْسَ مِنِّي

(البخاري ومسلم)

By God I fear Allah and I am more God-conscious than you. But I fast and break fast as well. I pray at night and sleep as well. I have also married. Whosoever forsakes my way is not from me.

(Bukhārī and Muslim)

In some religions and philosophies it is stressed that real spiritual heights can only be reached by living the life of an ascetic. One should retire in seclusion to contemplate and meditate so that one can achieve nearness to one's Creator. One should live in poverty and deprive oneself of everything so that salvation is attained. Some Christian traditions prescribe celibacy and in Hindu and Buddhist religions *sādhūs* and *bhakshūs* renounce the world and wander around begging and living in hardship. Aspects of such asceticism have also crept into some Sufi orders.

In Islam there is no conflict between body and soul. If the body is ill the soul will be restless. In some religions the way to achieve salvation is to torture the flesh. People think they can only achieve nearness to God by suppressing their natural desires. Islam is akin to man's natural life. It teaches us self-control and not self-torture. Thus suicide, self-mutilation or bodily harm are all unlawful acts. The highest priority according to Islam is self-preservation. Islam even allows the eating and drinking of unlawful things in order to save life.

What is our relationship with ourselves? All our energies and capabilities are given by Allah (*swt*) and we are not the owners of ourselves but rather only the trustees of our bodies and faculties. So we are not allowed to misuse or waste them. All our faculties and capabilities are necessary for our existence. Nothing is superfluous or bad in its essence. If we use them properly we will serve humanity. If we abuse them we will wreck our own lives on this earth as well as in the Hereafter.

The important thing is to know oneself. This self-knowledge is the key to understanding everything else in the universe. There is a saying, sometimes wrongly attributed to the Prophet (*ṣaws*), that one who knows himself knows his Lord. In this way a person knows his own position in respect of all other things. In this microcosm the whole macrocosm is reflected. All philosophers who have reflected deeply on this aspect of life arrived at the same conclusion. Socrates, the most eminent philosopher of all times, said: "O man! You should know yourself." Plato went still further by saying: "The souls of human beings were made aware of everything before they came into this world. Yet they became forgetful. This remembrance and reminder is necessary to create awakening." The Holy Qur'ān records that before each human being came to earth their souls accepted *tawḥīd* and the Lordship of Allah.

وَإِذْ أَخَذَ رَبُّكَ مِن بَنِيٓ ءَادَمَ مِن ظُهُورِهِمْ ذُرِّيَّتَهُمْ وَأَشْهَدَهُمْ عَلَىٰٓ
أَنفُسِهِمْ أَلَسْتُ بِرَبِّكُمْ قَالُوا بَلَىٰ شَهِدْنَآ ... ﴿١٧٢﴾

And recall when your Lord brought forth descendants from the loins of the sons of Adam and made them witnesses against their own selves, asking them "Am I not your Lord?" They said "Yes we do testify."

(al-A'rāf 7: 172)

Aristotle said: "If a man can unearth all the treasures from within himself, this will be quite sufficient for him." All later philosophers and scholars have expressed similar opinions. Rūmī, the celebrated Persian poet of the thirteenth century, asserted:

Look at me and unless you have insight into me
Surely you will be unaware of the Divine sparkle.

'Allāmah Iqbāl, the poet-philosopher of the last century, following his spiritual guide Rūmī propounded the concept of *khūdī* meaning self-realisation and self-knowledge to uplift the Muslim *Ummah* from its depth of self-doubt and backwardness. He asserted that it is only through *khūdī* that the human being can control all the forces of nature and create his own destiny. This life is just the stepping stone on the road to eternity. According to Iqbāl, *khūdī* creates self-respect and self-reliance in human beings thus releasing a person's potential to achieve success. He exhorts us to raise the level of *khūdī* to such heights that Allah consults His servants in determining their destiny.

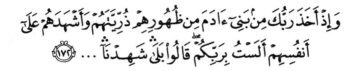

Self-recognition leads us to self-respect. It means we have self-esteem and we live with dignity. It is no virtue to live like a pauper when Allah has given someone enough means to live comfortably. It is not against *taqwā* (piety) to wear beautiful clothes and eat good food. In fact it is essential that we enjoy Allah's bounties and display His favours. Indeed the Prophet (*ṣaws*) said:

إِنَّ اللَّهَ جَمِيلٌ يُحِبُّ الْجَمَالَ (مسلم)

Allah is Beautiful and He loves beauty.

(Muslim)

Once a Companion came to the Prophet wearing ordinary and inferior quality clothes. The Prophet (*ṣaws*) asked him: "Do you have any possessions?" He replied: "I have much wealth. I have camels, cows, goats and horses as well as slaves." The Prophet observed:

فَإِذَا آتَاكَ اللَّهُ مَالاً فَلْيُرَ أَثَرُهُ عَلَيْكَ

(مشكاة المصابيح)

When Allah has bestowed so much wealth upon you then the signs of His favours and bounties should also be reflected in your lifestyle.

(*Mishkāt*)

Similarly once a person came to the mosque with unkempt hair. The Prophet suggested that he should go back and comb his hair properly (*Mishkāt*).

Self-respect does not mean that one should be proud and haughty. Pride is a characteristic of Satan, who is accursed because of his pride. Hence we should have humility. But showing off excessive humility is not right either. Once 'Umar ibn al-Khaṭṭāb saw a person walking very meekly; he asked him: "Why are you walking like this? You should walk properly and upright."

Self-respect means realising that we are the representatives of God on earth, and that we have to perform this task diligently and with dignity. The Holy Qur'ān says that we have been created in the best form (al-Tīn 95: 4), and that Allah has honoured us and given us superiority over other creations (al-Isrā' 17: 70). Hence we should not debase ourselves. Unless we respect ourselves no one else will respect us. Self-respect also means that we value our judgement and our honour. We have principles we stand by and we cannot be bought by bribe or influence. We see so many people having high principles yet they are tempted to sell their principles for a few worldly goods. Above all we should always listen to the voice of our conscience and never try to suppress its strictures. Furthermore, we must never try to justify our wrongful actions. If we did so our consciences would become weak and eventually die and we would be left without guidance. We should always try to keep our conscience healthy and alive. This conscience (*nafs lawwāmah*) is our safeguard that keeps us from persisting in sin and wrongful deeds.

Allah has endowed us with many talents. We have been given the potential to achieve what we want to achieve. Hence whatever capabilities are given to us we should try to enhance by training and hard work. We should constantly try to increase our hidden talents. The Prophet (*ṣaws*) is reported to have said that our today should be better than our yesterday. We should always aim high and make an effort to reach our goal.

As human beings we are liable to make mistakes. Wise people are those who learn from their mistakes and shortcomings. Therefore we should always take account of our deeds. 'Umar ibn al-Khaṭṭāb used to say: "Take account of yourself before your account is taken. Be ready for the big ground. Surely the account on the Day of Judgement will be easier for those who used to scrutinise themselves in this world." (Tirmidhī)

The Holy Qur'ān exhorts us:

يَٰٓأَيُّهَا ٱلَّذِينَ ءَامَنُوا۟ ٱتَّقُوا۟ ٱللَّهَ وَلْتَنظُرْ نَفْسٌ مَّا قَدَّمَتْ لِغَدٍ ... ﴿١٨﴾

O you who believe! Fear Allah. And let everyone scrutinise what he has sent forth for tomorrow.

(al-Ḥashr 59: 18)

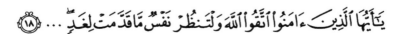

This self-assessment and self-criticism should be our regular habit. This can be done every night before going to bed. Do not be lenient with yourself. Don't give yourself any allowances. If you have committed any sin or mistake seek forgiveness from Allah. If you have oppressed or abused someone then you should seek their forgiveness as well and try to compensate them. We should develop this habit of introspectively probing ourselves. If we know ourselves we will know others as well as our Lord.

So let us pray that Allah (*swt*) may give us the courage to see our shortcomings and seek forgiveness for them. May He give us insight into our own selves and may we live with dignity and honour.

(*Āmīn*)

Further Reading

– Mawlānā Amīn Aḥsan Iṣlāḥī: 'Self-development in the Context of Man's Relationship with Allah'. In: Abdur Rashid Siddiqui (ed.), *Tazkiyah: The Islamic Path of Self-Development.* Markfield: The Islamic Foundation, 2004

Death and Disaster

تَبَٰرَكَ ٱلَّذِى بِيَدِهِ ٱلْمُلْكُ وَهُوَ عَلَىٰ كُلِّ شَىْءٍ قَدِيرٌ ﴿١﴾ ٱلَّذِى خَلَقَ ٱلْمَوْتَ
وَٱلْحَيَوٰةَ لِيَبْلُوَكُمْ أَيُّكُمْ أَحْسَنُ عَمَلًا ۚ وَهُوَ ٱلْعَزِيزُ ٱلْغَفُورُ ﴿٢﴾

Blessed be He in Whose hands is the Sovereignty, and He has power over all things. He has created death and life that He might test you as which of you is best in deed; and He is the Exalted in Might, Oft-Forgiving.

(al-Mulk 67: 1-2)

Every day people die in plane and train crashes or in car accidents all over the world. Then there are natural disasters like earthquakes, cyclones, hurricanes and droughts that claim thousands of lives at frequent intervals. Accidental deaths and disasters send shock waves of grief and mourning across families and nations. The type of questions people often ask when such things happen include. "Why do these disasters happen?" "Why has this happened to us?" Often people try to find physical causes for these events. If only the train driver had not jumped the red light this would not have happened. If only drivers were not going so fast then accidents could be averted. If the car drivers were more careful accidents could be avoided. If such and such precautions had been taken this would not have happened. These explanations miss the real purpose of such events. The Prophet (*ṣaws*) said:

وَإِيَّاكَ وَاللَّوْ فَإِنَّ لَوْ تَفْتَحُ عَمَلَ الشَّيْطَانِ (مسلم)

Beware of the word 'if' as it opens the door to the work of Satan.

(Muslim)

Allah (*swt*) says:

يَقُولُونَ لَوْ كَانَ لَنَا مِنَ ٱلْأَمْرِ شَىْءٌ مَّا قُتِلْنَا هَـٰهُنَا ۗ قُل لَّوْ كُنتُمْ فِى بُيُوتِكُمْ
لَبَرَزَ ٱلَّذِينَ كُتِبَ عَلَيْهِمُ ٱلْقَتْلُ إِلَىٰ مَضَاجِعِهِمْ ۖ ... ﴿١٥٤﴾

They say (to themselves): "If we had had anything to do with this affair we should not have been in the slaughter here." Say: "Even if you had remained in your homes, those to whom death was decreed would certainly have gone forth to the place of their death."

(Āl ʿImrān 3: 154)

In subsequent verses it is made very clear that Allah has the sole power over life and death:

يَـٰٓأَيُّهَا ٱلَّذِينَ ءَامَنُوا۟ لَا تَكُونُوا۟ كَٱلَّذِينَ كَفَرُوا۟ وَقَالُوا۟ لِإِخْوَٰنِهِمْ إِذَا ضَرَبُوا۟
فِى ٱلْأَرْضِ أَوْ كَانُوا۟ غُزًّى لَّوْ كَانُوا۟ عِندَنَا مَا مَاتُوا۟ وَمَا قُتِلُوا۟ لِيَجْعَلَ ٱللَّهُ
ذَٰلِكَ حَسْرَةً فِى قُلُوبِهِمْ ۗ وَٱللَّهُ يُحْىِۦ وَيُمِيتُ ۗ وَٱللَّهُ بِمَا تَعْمَلُونَ بَصِيرٌ ﴿١٥٦﴾

O you who believe! Be not like the unbelievers, who say of their brethren when they are travelling through the earth or engaged in fighting: "If they had stayed with us, they would not have died, or been slain." This that Allah may make it a cause of sighs and regrets in their hearts. It is Allah that gives life and death. And Allah sees well all that you do.

(Āl ʿImrān 3: 156)

Of course we should be careful while driving a car or travelling on a train. We should be prudent in taking all the precautions humanly possible. Yet what has been ordained cannot be averted. Even in train crashes some people die while others escape unhurt or slightly bruised. In earthquakes hundreds die yet sometimes a few are recovered alive after many days. Then people say how lucky they were to escape death. What is this luck? Rather this is their destiny that Allah has ordained. Both our life and our death is in Allah's (*swt)* hand.

Death is something that is inevitable and it is the most predictable event. In the Holy Qur'ān death is referred to as *Yaqīn* (certainty) because death is the most certain event in life. Allah categorically states in the Holy Qur'ān:

كُلُّ نَفْسٍ ذَآئِقَةُ ٱلْمَوْتِ ... ﴿١٨٥﴾

Every soul shall taste death.

(Āl 'Imrān 3: 185)

No one can escape death. It can come about at any time and any place. It can be sudden. It can be in a crowd or it can be in seclusion. It can be on the battlefield or it may be on a hospital bed where all the sophisticated life-saving apparatus and world-renowned doctors and physicians are available to save life. As Allah warns us in the Holy Qur'ān:

أَيْنَمَا تَكُونُوا۟ يُدْرِككُّمُ ٱلْمَوْتُ وَلَوْ كُنتُمْ فِى بُرُوجٍ مُّشَيَّدَةٍ ... ﴿٧٨﴾

Wherever you are death will find you out, even if you are in towers built up strong and high.

(al-Nisā' 4: 78)

James Shirley, a seventeenth-century English poet, beautifully conveyed the eventuality of death in his poem *Death: the Leveller*:

The glories of our blood and state,
Are shadows, not substantial things;
There is no armour against fate;
Death lays his icy hands on Kings,
Sceptre and Crown
Must tumble down
And in the dust be equal made,
With the poor crooked scythe and spade.

When someone dies suddenly, people say it is an untimely death. We should realise that the time of everyone's death is ordained and that it will come neither early nor late.

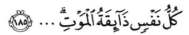

وَمَا كَانَ لِنَفْسٍ أَن تَمُوتَ إِلَّا بِإِذْنِ ٱللَّهِ كِتَٰبًا مُّؤَجَّلًا ... ﴿١٤٥﴾

Nor can a soul die except by Allah's leave,
the term being fixed as by writing.

(Āl ʿImrān 3: 145)

وَلِكُلِّ أُمَّةٍ أَجَلٌ فَإِذَا جَآءَ أَجَلُهُمْ لَا يَسْتَأْخِرُونَ سَاعَةً وَلَا يَسْتَقْدِمُونَ ﴿٣٤﴾

To every people is a term appointed: when their term is reached, not an hour can they cause delay, nor (an hour) can they advance (it in anticipation).

(al-Aʿrāf 7: 34)

Furthermore, our place of death is also ordained.

وَمَا تَدْرِى نَفْسٌ بِأَىِّ أَرْضٍ تَمُوتُ إِنَّ ٱللَّهَ عَلِيمٌ خَبِيرٌ ﴿٣٤﴾

Nor does anyone know in what land he is to die. Verily with Allah is full knowledge and He is acquainted (with all things).

(Luqmān 31: 34)

When death occurs all communication with this world is disconnected. We lose control over everything. We may have millions of pounds in our bank account but we cannot even sign a cheque. Hence the wise are those who are ready to meet death and who make preparations for their death. Allah exhorts us:

وَأَنفِقُوا۟ مِن مَّا رَزَقْنَٰكُم مِّن قَبْلِ أَن يَأْتِىَ أَحَدَكُمُ ٱلْمَوْتُ فَيَقُولَ رَبِّ لَوْلَآ
أَخَّرْتَنِىٓ إِلَىٰٓ أَجَلٍ قَرِيبٍ فَأَصَّدَّقَ وَأَكُن مِّنَ ٱلصَّٰلِحِينَ ﴿١٠﴾

And spend something (in charity) out of the substance which We have bestowed on you, before death should come to any of you and he should say, "O my Lord! Why did You not give me

respite for a while? I should then have given (largely) in charity, and I should have been one of the doers of good."
(al-Munāfiqūn 63: 10)

Shaddād ibn Aws, a Companion, narrates that the Prophet (*ṣaws*) said:

The really wise person is one who controls his self and works for the life after death.
(Tirmidhī)

James Shirley too echoes the same message in his poem:

Your heads must come,
To the cold tomb;
Only the actions of the just
Smell sweet, and blossom in their dust.

Whatever Allah does there is some purpose behind it. There is *ḥikmah* (wisdom) in all His actions, which is not manifestly clear to us. Maybe the pain we feel in bereavement is a subtle reminder to us that ultimately we all have to return to Allah. In this life: there is happiness and grief; there is poverty and prosperity; there is authority and there is subjugation; there is power and there is weakness; there is health and there is illness; there is progress and there is devastation. In all these situations there are tests for us so that Allah (*swt*) can ascertain whether we are predisposed towards *shukr* (gratefulness) or pride, tyranny, and intoxication by power. In other words, whether or not we are slaves to our carnal selves. Similarly, in bad times do we exercise *ṣabr* (patience and perseverance) or become depressed and despondent and use illegal means to achieve our gains. The Prophet (*ṣaws*) said:

There is a strange case with a believer. His affairs are full of benefits throughout and this is the case with a *Mu'min* only and no one else. If he is the recipient of happiness and pleasure and he is thankful this is beneficial to him. If he is afflicted with pain and misery and he is patient this is beneficial to him as well.
(Tirmidhī)

Natural disasters are often referred to as "Acts of God" even in the secular world. The fact is that all acts are Acts of God. Nothing happens in this world without His permission and knowledge. What for us are accidents and unforeseen disasters are in Allah's knowledge beforehand. So why do these events happen? There are two reasons. One is mentioned in the verse I recited at the start of this *khuṭbah* that these are a test to determine who is best in their deeds. The other reason is that these events are reminders to us of that Major Calamity which is going to engulf the whole world one day. People should take heed from these reminders and reform their lives.

We should also realise that events which occur in our lives have moral causes as well. The Prophet (*ṣaws*) warned that:

خَمْسٌ إِذَا ابْتُلِيْتُمْ بِهِنَّ وَأَعُوذُ بِاللَّهِ أَنْ تُدْرِكُوهُنَّ، لَمْ تَظْهَرِ الْفَاحِشَةُ فِي قَوْمٍ قَطُّ حَتَّى يُعْلِنُوا بِهَا إِلاَّ فَشَا فِيهِمُ الطَّاعُونُ وَالأَوْجَاعُ الَّتِي لَمْ تَكُنْ مَضَتْ فِي أَسْلاَفِهِمْ الَّذِينَ مَضَوْا، وَلَمْ يَنْقُصُوا الْمِكْيَالَ وَالْمِيزَانَ إِلاَّ أُخِذُوا بِالسِّنِينَ وَشِدَّةِ الْمَئُونَةِ وَجَوْرِ السُّلْطَانِ عَلَيْهِمْ، وَلَمْ يَمْنَعُوا زَكَاةَ أَمْوَالِهِمْ إِلاَّ مُنِعُوا الْقَطْرَ مِنَ السَّمَاءِ وَلَوْلاَ الْبَهَائِمُ لَمْ يُمْطَرُوا، وَلَمْ يَنْقُضُوا عَهْدَ اللَّهِ وَعَهْدَ رَسُولِهِ إِلاَّسَلَّطَ اللَّهُ عَلَيْهِمْ عَدُوًّا مِنْ غَيْرِهِمْ فَأَخَذُوا بَعْضَ مَا فِي أَيْدِيهِمْ وَمَا لَمْ تَحْكُمْ أَئِمَّتُهُمْ بِكِتَابِ اللَّهِ وَيَتَخَيَّرُوا مِمَّا أَنْزَلَ اللَّهُ إِلاَّجَعَلَ اللَّهُ بَأْسَهُمْ بَيْنَهُمْ

(البيهقي وابن ماحة)

There are five sins in which if people are involved it penetrates through into society and this is fatal. I seek Allah's refuge from these evils spreading amongst you. If fornication and adultery are openly prevalent then such diseases will inflict you, which were not there before. If people cheat by measuring short then Allah will impose drought on them and they will become the targets of oppressive regimes. When people stop paying *zakāh*, then

> rainfall is curtailed. Then there will be no rainfall if there are no animals and birds in the locality. When insurgency and breaking of covenants with Allah occurs then Allah imposes non-Muslim enemies upon them who usurp a lot from them. And finally, if Muslim rulers do not govern according to the Book of Allah then Allah imposes disunity in the Muslim society and they start killing each other.
>
> (Bayhaqī and Ibn Mājah)

If we were to survey our society we would see that many evil practices are prevalent among us. Unless we reform ourselves and are subservient to our Creator all sorts of disasters will befall us. We should return with humility to our Lord and do *istighfār* (repentance) to Him so that He may open the gates of His Mercy to us and save us from all disasters.

(*Āmīn*)

Despondency

وَلَا تَا۟يْـَٔسُوا۟ مِن رَّوْحِ ٱللَّهِ ۖ إِنَّهُۥ لَا يَا۟يْـَٔسُ مِن رَّوْحِ ٱللَّهِ إِلَّا ٱلْقَوْمُ ٱلْكَـٰفِرُونَ ﴿٨٧﴾

And never give up hope of Allah's soothing Mercy – truly no one despairs of Allah's soothing Mercy except those who have no faith.

(Yūsuf 12: 87)

لَا تَقْنَطُوا۟ مِن رَّحْمَةِ ٱللَّهِ ... ﴿٥٣﴾

Despair not of the Mercy of Allah.

(al-Zumar 39: 53)

The Muslim *Ummah* is passing through a very crucial time in its history. Muslims are subjugated, humiliated and overawed by the forces of their adversaries. They are divided, disintegrated, feeling low, weak and uncertain. Muslim governments are under the domination of an elite group of Western-educated oligarchs or hereditary rulers who are manipulated by different world powers. They in turn undermine the revival of Islamic teachings and culture, and in this way the Muslim *Ummah* is torn apart from within as well. Infighting on issues of nationality, language, schools of *fiqh*, race, etc., is rampant in the Muslim societies of many countries.

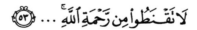

Seeing this situation people become very despondent. In their despair they adopt strategies to reverse the situation which are futile and may violate Islamic teachings. To start with, to be despondent is a very dangerous disease. It is like a cancer that destroys the body's cells. Yet how can we Muslims be desperate when we believe in Allah and His Mercy?

To come out of this spiral of despondency and despair we require knowledge and insight as well as courage and determination. I agree the situation of the Muslim *Ummah* is very serious and painful to talk about. Yet we have to have hope. It is only unbelievers who have lost hope in Allah's Mercy.

The word *Iblīs*, the other name for Satan, comes from the root that means one who has lost hope. Whereas Adam after making his mistake repented and sought forgiveness, *Iblīs* was arrogant and rebelled, thus losing hope in Allah's Mercy. Although the situation of our *Ummah* at present is precarious we should be hopeful that it will change for the better. By being hopeful I do not mean we close our eyes to the facts and live in a fool's paradise. Or behave like an ostrich and bury our heads in the sand. We have to work hard and hope that with our very humble efforts we can bring about change in our society; just like a very dim light in a very dark room can illuminate the way to salvation. If we work sincerely and wholeheartedly with hope we will *Inshā' Allāh* see the results.

We have the example of our Prophet (peace be upon him) when he left Ṭā'if bruised and injured. Yet he said I am not despondent. A new generation will come and they will worship Allah. If our Prophet can hope and pray that Abū Jahl or ʿUmar who were enemies of Islam can become Muslims, why can't we be hopeful that *īmān* will grace our enemies? If the descendants of Halākū Khān can become Muslims why should we be despondent when it is possible that those who are persecuting us will eventually become people of the faith? We have to follow the lead given by our illustrious predecessors. To illustrate this point Sayyid Abu'l Ḥasan ʿAlī Nadwī related an historical event in his book, *Daʿwah in The West: the Qur'ānic Paradigm*. The following is an abridged version of what he wrote:

> After the Tartars overran Baghdad and destroyed the ʿAbbāsid *Khilāfah*, one of their rulers was Tuqluq Tīmūr Khān (1347-1363). Once he was out hunting and camped in the game reserve that was secluded on all sides. A wandering Persian, Shaykh Jamāl al-Dīn

unwittingly trespassed into his Camp. The Khān's soldiers arrested him and brought him before Tuqluq Tīmūr. He became furious and contemptuously asked the Shaykh: "Who is more worthy a dog or a Persian?" To this the Shaykh replied: "It cannot be decided here and now. If I die in a state of *īmān* (faith) I am more worthy, otherwise this dog is more worthy than me." The Khān became intrigued and asked him about his faith. The Shaykh then set before him the doctrines of Islam with such fervour and zeal that the heart of the Khān that before had been as hard as stone melted like wax. The Khān was very much impressed by this sincere explanation of Islam. He said: "Bear with me a little, and when I have entered into possession of the kingdom of my forefathers, come to me again." Shaykh Jamāl al-Dīn did not live to see Tuqluq Tīmūr's victory. However, he told the details of his encounter to his son, Shaykh Rashīd al-Dīn and asked him to approach Tuqluq Tīmūr if he became a King and to tell him that he had died in a state of *īmān* and to remind him of the incident. After a few years Shaykh Rashīd al-Dīn heard that Tīmūr had finally defeated his rivals and had been proclaimed king. He set out to meet the king but when he approached his palace he was stopped by his guards as he was a scruffy-looking beggar. Shaykh Rashīd al-Dīn thought of a scheme to attract the King's attention. He camped outside the palace and started giving *Adhān* every day at dawn. This disturbed the King's sleep and he asked his guards to arrest the offender. The Shaykh was brought before the King, and reminded him about his encounter with his father, saying: "I am here to testify that my father died in a state of *īmān*." Thereafter Tuqluq Tīmūr Khān accepted Islam and with him all his courtiers and subjects. This historical event is recorded both by Thomas Arnold in his *Preaching of Islam* as well as in Persian and Turkish sources.

So this is the task that we have to undertake to bring about a change in our situation. Our mission in this world is the same as the Prophet's (*ṣaws*) mission: to convey the message of Islam to humanity. This *Ummah* has been given this trust (*amānah*) to carry forward the responsibility that was given to the Prophet (*ṣaws*). We are honoured in the Qur'ān as *khaira ummatin* (the best *Ummah*) whose duty is to be a witness unto mankind and a witness unto truth. The greatest challenge before us is to propagate the message of Islam to most people of this world.

These days if you ask someone to do *da'wah* work they say how bad these times are and that nobody listens. We should realise that we are responsible for *da'wah* – to bring humanity to the path of righteousness. It is our prime duty and for performing this duty there are tremendous rewards:

مَنْ دَعَا إِلَى هُدًى كَانَ لَهُ مِنَ ٱلأَجْرِ مِثْلُ أُجُورِ مَنْ تَبِعَهُ

(مسلم)

One who guides someone to the right path will have the reward of all those who follow it.

(Muslim)

فَوَاللَّهِ لَأَنْ يَهْدِيَ اللَّهُ بِكَ رَجُلاً خَيْرٌ لَكَ مِنْ أَنْ يَكُونَ لَكَ حُمْرُ النَّعَمِ

(البخاري)

Just to guide someone to the right path is more profitable than a red flock of camels.

(Bukhārī and Muslim)

The best armour and trickery which Satan uses against us is to create despondency and despair. He knows that once we are on the slippery slope of despair the spiral will take us down and under.

To embark on the mission of reforming society is a very daunting task. We encounter many failures and setbacks. In all other affairs of the world we can with some certainty predict the results of our efforts. But in reforming an individual or to bring about change in society we have to tackle very unpredictable situations.

We can mould iron and steel by our determination and dexterity. But how can one mould the hardened human heart? We know we can bring out gold from the gold mine. But how can we transform a wicked person into an adorable human being? We know we can sow wheat or barley and will be able to harvest it. But can we be certain to inculcate qualities of truthfulness, mercy and kindness in human souls? We can build a strong wall by putting one brick on the other and joining them with mortar. But can we harmonise the thinking and actions of different individuals? We know when the darkness of night will end and the new dawn appear. But can we predict when doubts of darkness will clear and the dawn of faith arise?

Satan, our arch enemy, from every nook and corner in different guises comes and makes us lose our hearts. Sometimes we think how can I a mere insignificant person reform this corrupt society; I am not well versed in the Islamic knowledge? But the Prophet (*ṣaws*) said convey from me even if you know one *āyah* (verse). Sometimes we make the excuse that we are not very pious and God-fearing but no one is perfect. Otherwise we would all have been angels. Instead we are human beings and we are all sinners. When we look around and see that not many people are engaged in this noble work and that the vast majority are ignorant and careless we say we cannot undertake such a huge task. Only the prophets and their companions were capable of such deeds.

As if God would abandon us from His Mercy and Justice and burden us with such a heavy load that we could not carry. We say this is a very bad time. There is so much materialism and self-interest in society. Few want to listen to talk of piety. Most are after material wealth and worldly goods. Issues of race, language and nationalism have divided our society. Some of our leaders are hypocrites. All they want is power. They want to enrich themselves. They look after their own interests. Much of society is corrupt and decadent.

We know that some hearts are like stones yet at times even stones break and water gushes out of them. Yes, it is possible for Allah to change people's hearts. Yes, we can witness the revival of Islam. But we must struggle to live a clean life and hope for Allah's Mercy.

Night only lingers on until the appearance of the glorious sun. Indeed the glorious sun has to break the mould of darkness. Let us pray that Allah may give us hope and courage to convey the message of Islam to the whole of humanity.

(*Āmīn*)

Happiness

يَٰٓأَيَّتُهَا ٱلنَّفْسُ ٱلْمُطْمَئِنَّةُ ﴿٢٧﴾ ٱرْجِعِىٓ إِلَىٰ رَبِّكِ رَاضِيَةً مَّرْضِيَّةً ﴿٢٨﴾
فَٱدْخُلِى فِى عِبَٰدِى ﴿٢٩﴾ وَٱدْخُلِى جَنَّتِى ﴿٣٠﴾

O you contented soul! Return to your Lord – well pleased (yourself) and well-pleasing unto Him! Enter you, then, among My servants! Indeed, enter you My Heaven.
(al-Fajr 89: 27-30)

Happiness is that elusive state of mind that is pursued and desired by everyone. The perception of a good life by many is a life of pleasure, in which you get what you want and want what you get. Hence the acquisition of wealth is considered to bring happiness to its owner. Living in an age of doubt and death as the final destination, no wonder people like to be surrounded by available pleasure. This Epicurean philosophy was proclaimed by Emperor Bābar in his famous line of Persian poetry: "Bābar indulge yourself in pleasure as this world will not exist again." This sums up the sentiments of many very well.

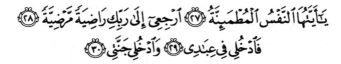

Of course, pleasure is always more desirable than a lack of it. Yet the pursuit of pleasure may entail doing wrong things – things that undermine our happiness, by diverting our emotions from the course that fulfils us. We get pleasure by fulfiling of desires, whereas happiness comes with a fulfilment of heart with contentment and tranquillity. Thus, even among the rich, the consensus is that wealth is not in itself a recipe for contentment. For some people it is a burden; a responsibility accompanied by a recurring fear of losing it. It was Pablo Picasso who once said "I would like to live like a poor man with lots of money", and it is lottery winners who will most often find themselves in this situation. Many wealthy people say: "No amount of money in the world can buy complete peace of mind." Recent research by two British academics, Robert Worcester of the London School of Economics and Nick Marks of Surrey University, into the link between personal spending power and perceived quality of life, showed that people in Bangladesh, one of the poorest countries in the world, attain more happiness from their small incomes than the British from their relatively large ones.

So how can we achieve happiness and tranquillity in our lives? First, we must know that we are human beings with needs, desires and appetites. And we are people, with goals, ambitions and ideals. We are different from other creatures as we are endowed with reason and are capable of making free and conscious choices. Unlike animals we seek fulfilment of the person rather than satisfaction of the body. Again, we are self-conscious and we do not merely do things. We have a conception of what we do and why. As rational beings we admire cardinal virtues: courage, justice, wisdom, prudence and temperance. Those who lack these virtues are unreliable. Allah (*swt*) through His Messengers and the Prophets has provided us with the means to acquire happiness. In one of the Psalms, the Prophet Dā'ūd (peace be upon him) said: "Happy is the man who fears the Lord, who is only too willing to follow His orders" (Psalm 112: 1). This wisdom imparted by the great Prophet is echoed in the writings of ancient philosophers who sincerely tried to pursue a seeking of the truth. Aristotle, the ancient Greek philosopher, made a sensible observation that happiness is an activity of the soul in accordance with virtue. Hence only the virtuous are happy.

So if happiness is the goal, why can't you get there by cheating? The reason is that while you can aim at pleasure, you cannot aim at happiness. You need other aims like values and ideals. Happiness only comes when we are content with what we have done. We should understand that happiness like love and friendship comes only when you do not aim at it. Even if we are wealthy, powerful or successful by dint of our cheating we are nonetheless still not happy. Cheating destroys self-esteem whereas happiness requires self-approval. This feeling of self-satisfaction is the message that is given by the Prophet Muḥammad (*ṣaws*):

إِذَا سَرَّتْكَ حَسَنَتُكَ وَسَاءَتْكَ سَيِّئَتُكَ فَأَنْتَ مُؤْمِنٌ (أحمد)

If you feel pleasure performing good deeds and feel remorse committing evil you are a true Muslim.

(Aḥmad)

The problem people in the West face is how to cultivate virtue in an age of dwindling religious faith. Even if Aristotle is right in thinking that we all have reason to cultivate virtue, his argument is beyond the reach of most people. What, therefore, inspires people to do what they should?

No doubt, as Plato conceded it is only religion that motivates them to do what they would otherwise not do. This fact is also acknowledged by the eminent modern philosopher Roger Scruton. He says that certain truths are only available to us through a religious concept of the world. Religion provides a sense of things as good in themselves, as ends rather than means. We seek happiness in the wrong place: the world has forgotten that virtue is the only path to contentment.

Our *nafs* (soul, self, ego) is composed of a complex mixture of opposing forces of good and evil. Man is given the choice of following the path of righteousness or to go the other way. As Allah (*swt*) says: "We showed him the way: whether he be grateful or ungrateful (rests on his will) (al-Insān 76: 3). We are all in a constant struggle against divergent forces. We are always liable to be swayed by temptations and commit sins. As the Prophet Yūsuf (peace be upon him) acknowledged when he was able to safeguard his chastity:

وَمَآ أُبَرِّئُ نَفْسِيٓ ۚ إِنَّ ٱلنَّفْسَ لَأَمَّارَةٌۢ بِٱلسُّوٓءِ إِلَّا مَا رَحِمَ رَبِّيٓ ۚ
إِنَّ رَبِّي غَفُورٌ رَّحِيمٌ ﴿٥٣﴾

Nor do I absolve my own self (of blame): the (human) soul is certainly prone to evil, unless my Lord bestows His Mercy: but surely my Lord is Oft-Forgiving, Most Merciful.

(Yūsuf 12: 53)

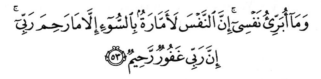

The *nafs* that tempts us to evil is called *nafs ammārah* (the imperious, carnal self). To protect us from the treachery of this aspect of our *nafs* there is *nafs lawwāmah* (the reproaching self) which we call conscience. When we commit a sin our conscience reproaches us for doing such a shameful act. Allah (*swt*) presented this as a proof of the Day of Resurrection (al-Qiyāmah 75: 2). If we listen to the voice of our conscience whenever we commit any sin and we retract and repent we return to the path of righteousness. But if we persist and suppress the voice of our conscience it becomes dead and we go down the slippery slope of doom. Those who resist the temptation and practise self-restraint accepting the dictates of their conscience attain the blessing of *nafs muṭma'innah* (the restful, contented self). This is the highest achievement for human beings. This is the stage when one is well-pleased and happy with one's Creator and He is well-pleased with you.

This soul state can only be achieved by remembrance of Allah (*swt*). As the Qur'ān states: "For no doubt in the remembrance of Allah do hearts find satisfaction" (al-Raʿd 13: 28). If we regularly remember Allah we will be saved from temptations of the soul and then it is easier to follow the path of guidance without hesitation and doubts. We will be ready and willing to face difficulties, sacrifice our desires and subjugate our passions for the sake of achieving self-satisfaction and the approval of our Lord. Thus, we will be rewarded by *sakīnah* (tranquillity) that fills the heart with sublime bliss. This is the gift that Allah bestowed on believers: "Allah sent down His tranquillity on His Messenger and to the believers, and made them close to the command of self-restraint; and well were they entitled to it and worthy of it" and, "It is He Who sent down tranquillity into the hearts of the believers..."(al-Fatḥ 48: 26 and 4). The Prophet (*ṣaws*) used to pray:

اللَّهُمَّ إِنِّي أَعُوذُ بِكَ مِنْ قَلْبٍ لاَ يَخْشَعُ وَمِنْ دُعَاءٍ لاَ يُسْمَعُ وَمِنْ
نَفْسٍ لاَ تَشْبَعُ وَمِنْ عِلْمٍ لاَ يَنْفَعُ

(أحمد)

> O Lord! I seek Your refuge from the heart that is fearless and the prayer that is not heard and the soul that is unsatisfied and knowledge that is not useful.
>
> (Aḥmad)

So let us pray: "O Merciful Lord! Our hearts are between Your finger grip; You may manipulate it, as You like. Please make our hearts submit to Your *Dīn* and make our hearts satisfied with Your remembrance and send down Your tranquillity on our hearts and keep us on the path of piety and make us worthy of it."

(*Āmīn*)

Sports and Leisure

وَأَعِدُّوا۟ لَهُم مَّا ٱسْتَطَعْتُم مِّن قُوَّةٍ ... ﴿٦٠﴾

Against them make ready your strength to the utmost of your power...

(al-Anfāl 8: 60)

Sport is the spice of life. It provides relaxation and entertainment. It relieves boredom and brings back a child-like delight in adults. Like anything else in life if it becomes an obsession then it degenerates into unhealthy rivalries, conflicts and friction. If it dominates our lives then instead of a pastime it becomes a waste of time. Instead of a game that is played for relaxation and fun it becomes a vehicle for achieving fame and enhancing national glory. Thus, instead of being the spice of life it destroys the very purpose of sport. It leads to unhealthy practices. Instead of fair competition participants resort to cheating and unfair practices even to taking drugs to enhance their performances.

What we see now is that sport has become more important than religion. Indeed it has become a religion. We have put sport on top of everything else. It has become a profession and big business. Sportsmen and women no longer play games as a pastime instead it has become the aim of their lives. We too have made sport the pivot of our lives, the goal of our existence. When we engross ourselves in sports and forget Allah then we forego Allah's Mercy and Grace and there is no guidance for us. Allah (*swt*) clearly states:

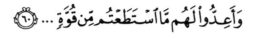

الَّذِينَ اتَّخَذُوا دِينَهُمْ لَهْوًا وَلَعِبًا وَغَرَّتْهُمُ الْحَيَاةُ الدُّنْيَا ۚ
فَالْيَوْمَ نَنسَاهُمْ كَمَا نَسُوا لِقَاءَ يَوْمِهِمْ هَٰذَا وَمَا كَانُوا
بِآيَاتِنَا يَجْحَدُونَ ﴿٥١﴾

Those who took their religion as an idle sport and a play and were deceived by the life of the world. So that day We shall forget them as they forgot the meeting of this day of theirs as they used to dispute Our signs.

(al-Aʿrāf 7: 51)

In another verse Allah categorically states that such actions will result in sealing our hearts and closing down our faculties of seeing and hearing.

أَفَرَأَيْتَ مَنِ اتَّخَذَ إِلَٰهَهُ هَوَاهُ وَأَضَلَّهُ اللَّهُ عَلَىٰ عِلْمٍ وَخَتَمَ عَلَىٰ سَمْعِهِ وَقَلْبِهِ وَجَعَلَ
عَلَىٰ بَصَرِهِ غِشَاوَةً فَمَن يَهْدِيهِ مِن بَعْدِ اللَّهِ ۚ أَفَلَا تَذَكَّرُونَ ﴿٢٣﴾

Have you seen him who takes as his god his own vain desire, and Allah has sent him astray despite his knowledge, and has sealed up his hearing and his heart and has set up a covering on his sight? Who, then will guide him after Allah (has withdrawn guidance)? Will you not then be admonished?

(al-Jāthiyah 45: 23)

True sport is not just winning. Victory is the objective, of course, since sport is competitive. But if winning alone becomes the goal, then morality and humanity are the victims. When victory, money and fame become so important then participants resort to unfair tactics like drug taking and cheating. The value of gold is tarnished and diminished.

In this mad rush for gaining gold medals there are very few athletes who care for their goal in life more than just winning. For example Jonathan Edwards, one of the greatest triple jumpers who won the gold medal at the Barcelona Olympics and the silver medal in Atlanta in 1992 and 1996 respectively, said: “Sometimes I lie in bed and think, I jump into a sand pit for a living. Am I doing anything worthwhile here? You see doctors in

Rwanda and think, they are making a difference, but I am jumping into a sand pit. Who benefits from that?" This is what all sane people who think and reflect on the realities of life should be asking, instead of being carried away by the euphoria created by media hype. Jonathan Edwards is a devout Christian who for many years refused to compete on a Sunday. How many Muslim cricketers voiced their objection to playing during the Friday Prayers? Jonathan is a family man and considers his wife and children more important than his fame. Here is a person, with whose faith we do not agree but who has got his priorities right. So why then doesn't he stop jumping? A vital question he himself raises. And he frankly admits that he loves his Mercedes with the personalised number plate. There is so much money to be made. Footballers earn millions of pounds. Their transfer from one club to another costs several millions! Yet there are millions of people all over the world facing starvation and death. Such huge amounts if used for constructive work could eliminate poverty and disease. But we enjoy our sport. But we do not consider the social cost we pay for this enjoyment. Football has become synonymous with hooliganism and racial abuse. Enormous amounts of money and police resources have to be mobilised to keep the peace and quiet. There is a lot of drinking and the resulting violence has paralysed our city centres. Then there is gambling on the outcome of results in most sporting events. Long and continuous cricket tours disrupt and damage family life and sometimes result in marriage break-ups. It may boost the income of pub owners but suspension of economic activity takes its toll elsewhere.

The Olympic Games, held every four years, have become a showpiece of jingoistic and nationalistic euphoria. It enacts the pagan rites of a modern decadent Western culture. Billions of pounds are spent on its organisation. There are hundreds of games in the competition some of which are so ludicrous that one wonders why on earth they are included in the programme. The reason is very obvious: the International Olympic Committee wants to maximise the amount it gets from all the various television networks.

So what guidance does Islam provide about this important activity in our lives. Briefly, we should note that first, Islam is a natural and practical way of life. It does not prescribe imaginary unachievable ideals. It is firmly rooted in the realities of life. Second, Islam does not regard human beings as angels. Thus, it accepts that people need relaxation, enjoyment, entertainment and leisure activities. Third, Islam does not require that we speak about nothing but piety or that we remain silent and meditate. It does not require that we listen to nothing but the recitation of the Holy Qur'ān and spend all our spare time in the mosques. Allah, our Creator knows that we have physical needs and desires. We want leisure and enjoyment in our lives.

Let me just briefly mention a few incidents from the *Sīrah* of the Prophet (*ṣaws*) who is the perfect model for us to follow. He spent time in prayer and meditation yet he also joined his Companions in small talk and jokes. He had a great sense of humour. It is reported by al-Tirmidhī that once an old woman came to him, saying: "O Messenger of Allah, pray to Allah that He admit me to *Jannah*." The Prophet (*ṣaws*) said: "O Mother of such and such person, no old woman will enter *Jannah*." She broke down and wept, supposing that she would not enter Paradise. The Prophet (*ṣaws*) then explained to her that no old woman would enter *Jannah* as an old woman, Allah would restore her youth and admit her to Paradise as a young virgin. He then recited to her the verse:

إِنَّآ أَنشَأْنَٰهُنَّ إِنشَآءً ﴿٣٥﴾ فَجَعَلْنَٰهُنَّ أَبْكَارًا ﴿٣٦﴾ عُرُبًا أَتْرَابًا ﴿٣٧﴾

We created (their companions) of special creation, and made them virgin-pure (and undefiled) – beloved (by nature), equal in age.

(al-Wāqi'ah 56: 35-37)

Shaykh Yūsuf al-Qaraḍāwī discussed this issue in his famous book *al-Ḥalāl wa'l-Ḥarām fi'l Islām* (The Lawful and the Prohibited in Islam). After quoting the above incident he went on to say:

> Following the Prophet's example his noble and pure Companions also enjoyed humour and laughter, play and sport, which relaxed their bodies and minds and prepared them the better to travel on the long, arduous path of striving in the cause of truth and justice. 'Alī ibn Abī Ṭālib said: "Minds get tired, as do bodies, so treat them with humour and refresh your minds from time to time, for a tired mind becomes blind." Another Companion, Abū Dardā'

said: "I entertain my heart with something trivial in order to make it stronger in the service of truth."

Accordingly, there is no harm in the Muslim's entertaining himself in order to relax his mind or refreshing himself with some permissible sport or play with his friends. However, the pursuit of pleasure should not become the goal of his life so that he devotes himself to it forgetting his religious obligations. Nor should he joke about serious matters. It has been aptly said: "Season your conversation with humour in the same way as you season your food with salt" (p.292).

Once the Prophet (*ṣaws*) and his wife *Umm al-Mu'minīn* 'Ā'ishah competed in a race. As 'Ā'ishah was younger and swifter she won the race. Then, later in life, both competed again but at that time 'Ā'ishah had put on weight and so the Prophet (*ṣaws*) won. He told his wife that this was revenge for his earlier defeat. The Prophet (*ṣaws*) was an accomplished wrestler. More than once he defeated a renowned wrestler called Rukānah, who was well-known for his physical strength and skill (Abū Dā'ūd and Aḥmad). The Prophet (*ṣaws)* also allowed some Abyssinians to display their skill with spears in the courtyard of his Mosque. The Prophet (*ṣaws*) further allowed *Umm al-Mu'minīn* 'Ā'ishah to watch their show.

Among other permissible sports are competition in archery or with other weapons and other skills like swimming and riding. Such sports are not just a hobby but more importantly constituted that kind of force which Allah has commended to be mustered:

وَأَعِدُّوا۟ لَهُم مَّا ٱسْتَطَعْتُم مِّن قُوَّةٍ ... ﴿٦٠﴾

Against them make ready your strength to the utmost of your power...

(al-Anfāl 8: 60)

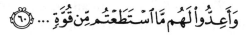

The Prophet (*ṣaws*) said: "Listen carefully there is strength in archery," (Muslim) and he repeated this three times. There are several such Traditions reported in authentic collections of *aḥādīth*, such as: Practise archery; it is good for you (al-Ṭabarānī). Practise archery and horseback riding (Muslim). Any action without the remembrance of Allah is either a diversion or heedlessness excepting four acts: walking from target to target (during archery practise), training a horse, playing with one's family and learning to swim (al-Ṭabarānī).

We can see that Islam wants us to live a balanced life. We should fulfil our duties to our Creator and we should earn a livelihood to support our families and enjoy our life as well.

So what are Muslim nations doing about sports? As in everything else the Muslim world is lagging behind in sport. We follow the agenda laid down by the West. We have no alternative strategy to follow. We do not hold sports as dictated by Islamic guidelines. We do not allow Muslim women to participate in sports. Muslim nations should follow the Islamic guidelines and hold sports for men and women separately. Thus helping them to attain fitness and compete for excellence in all permissible sports and games that are useful for human beings, avoiding commercial exploitation and frivolous competition. Unless we present the alternative options the world together with the rest of the Muslim world will be dragged along the path of ruin where Western capitalist society seems to want to take us.

Let us pray that Allah may give us the courage to follow the guidance of Islam in all spheres of our lives.

(*Āmīn*)

Human Rights

يَٰٓأَيُّهَا ٱلنَّاسُ إِنَّا خَلَقْنَٰكُم مِّن ذَكَرٍ وَأُنثَىٰ وَجَعَلْنَٰكُمْ شُعُوبًا وَقَبَآئِلَ لِتَعَارَفُوٓا۟ ۚ
إِنَّ أَكْرَمَكُمْ عِندَ ٱللَّهِ أَتْقَىٰكُمْ ۚ إِنَّ ٱللَّهَ عَلِيمٌ خَبِيرٌ ﴿١٣﴾

O mankind! We created you from a single (pair) of male and female, and made you into nations and tribes, that you may know each other. Verily the most honoured of you in the sight of Allah is (he who is) the most righteous of you. And Allah has full knowledge and is well-acquainted (with all things).

(al-Ḥujurāt 49: 13)

The equality of human beings was proclaimed by Islam long before the advent of the French Revolution's slogan of "Liberty, Equality and Fraternity" in the eighteenth century. The Holy Qur'ān declares that mankind is descended from one pair (Adam and Hawwā' – peace be upon them). The division of tribes, races and nations are convenient labels to identify them. They are not designed to create a sense of superiority. The same message was reinforced by the Prophet (*ṣaws*) in his last sermon on the Day of 'Arafah on the Mount of Mercy, where he declared that there is no superiority of Arabs over non-Arabs or whites over non-whites and vice versa. All are descendants of Adam and Adam was made of clay.

This was truly a charter for human rights, one unequivocally declared centuries before the Universal Declaration of Human Rights drafted by the United Nations or the Charter on Human Rights by the Council of Europe. The guiding principles of Islam governed social, political and human rights. These rights are the right to life, the protection of honour, freedom of expression and religion and equality before the law and many others. These rights are available not only to Muslims but are to be enjoyed by the whole of humanity.

Today we see violations of human rights regularly committed all over the world by the very nations that were the signatories to the human rights charters. Unfortunately, Muslims are singled out for inhumane treatment in many parts of the world. These defenceless Muslims are subjected to torture, terror and humiliation. The abuse of human rights committed by the Serbs in Bosnia and Kosovo, by Israelis in Palestine and by the Indians in Kashmir is well documented. Despite protests against them and resolutions passed against the atrocities in various forums all over the world their plight remains still horrific. Many reports by several international human rights organisations condemning such barbaric acts do not even bring about change. There would appear then to be no effective mechanism for enforcing human rights.

By contrast, we have the shining examples of the lives of the Companions: how they incorporated the teachings of Islam when formulating Islamic State policies in times of peace and war. Abū Bakr Ṣiddīq, the first *Khalīfah* (may Allah be pleased with him), when sending the first expedition to Syria instructed his commanders to follow the principles of justice and moderation. He told them:

> Be just, break not your pledge of faith, mutilate none, slay neither children, old men nor women; injure not the date palm nor burn it with fire; nor cut down any fruit-bearing tree, slay neither flocks nor herds nor camels, except for food; you may perchance come across men who have retired into monasteries, leave them and their works in peace.

This illustrates the emphasis on human rights during a time of war in an age when there were no Red Cross or Geneva Convention.

The attitude and activities of the Khawārij (an extremist faction of Muslims) during the *khilāfah* of ʿAlī ibn Abī Ṭālib (may Allah be pleased with him) are well known to those who have read Islamic history. They used to abuse the *Khalīfah* openly, and threaten to murder him. When some of them were arrested for threatening to commit murder and were brought before ʿAlī, he set them free, telling his officers: "As long as they do not actually perpetrate offences against the state, the mere use of abusive language or the threat of the use of force are not such offences for which they can be imprisoned." Imām Abū Ḥanīfah recorded the following saying from ʿAlī: "As long as they do not set out on armed rebellion, the *Khalīfah* of the Faithful will not interfere with them." On another occasion ʿAlī was delivering a lecture in the mosque when some Khārjīs raised their special slogan. ʿAlī said: "We will not deny you the right to come to the mosques to worship God, nor will we not give you your share from the wealth of the state as long as you are with us. We shall never take military action against you as long as you do not fight with us." One can visualise the tough opposition that ʿAlī faced. It was a more violent and vociferous opposition than that faced by any present-day democratic state. Yet the freedom that he allowed to the opposition was such that it has no parallel in history. The threat was real as we know and that the Khawārij in the end did assassinate him. Yet he did not arrest even those who threatened him with murder nor did he imprison them.

Amongst the rights that Islam confers on human beings is the right to protest against government tyranny. The Holy Qur'ān says:

لَّا يُحِبُّ ٱللَّهُ ٱلْجَهْرَ بِٱلسُّوٓءِ مِنَ ٱلْقَوْلِ إِلَّا مَن ظُلِمَ ۚ
وَكَانَ ٱللَّهُ سَمِيعًا عَلِيمًا ﴿١٤٨﴾

God does not like speaking evil talk publicly unless one has been wronged.

(al-Nisā' 4: 148)

This means that Allah strongly disapproves of abusive language or strong words of condemnation, but if someone has been the victim of injustice or tyranny, God gives him the right to openly protest against that injury. The right is not limited to individuals only. The words are general. Therefore if an individual, group, or party after assuming the reins of authority begins to terrorise individuals, then the whole population has the right to raise the voice of protest against it. This is a God-given right. No one has the authority to deny it. Those who do deny this right rebel against God.

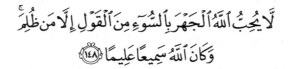

The tragedy we face is that Muslim governments themselves are equally guilty of torture, inhumane treatment and the heaping of humiliation on fellow Muslims. They are not ashamed and fearful of Allah when they violate the laws and teachings of Islam. The very laws that give them legitimacy to govern also bestow rights upon citizens. The sanctity of a Muslim's blood, his property and his honour were declared by the Prophet (*ṣaws*) as sacred as the 10th of Dhu'l Ḥijjah – the day of Sacrifice, the month of *Ḥajj* and the City of Makkah. The Muslim should protest and strive against oppression everywhere, even if it involves challenging the highest authority in the state.

The behaviour of Muslim governments is deplorable in this respect. We usually criticise the West for the very many evil things that happen here. But at least their record on human rights is better than that of so-called Muslim countries. Some Muslim governments even try to blackmail Western countries, persuading them to refuse the right of asylum to those who are fleeing from persecution. Whereas under Islamic law: "Every persecuted or oppressed person has the right to seek refuge and asylum. This right is guaranteed to every human being irrespective of race, religion, colour and sex." I am quoting here from the Universal Islamic Declaration of Human Rights prepared by the Islamic Council of Europe.

Islamic teachings require us to treat everyone fairly. If a person or a group commits an atrocity against us, it is not permissible to attribute the blame on all persons of that race, religion or nationality. We know Israel and India are persecuting Muslims in Palestine and Kashmir. Yet we should not make Jews and Hindus responsible for the acts of their states. The suffering of the Muslims at the hands of the Jewish State has created great hostility. This has spilled over into hating Jews generally. We should remember that Islam honoured them as People of the Book and if Israel is violating the human rights of Palestinians it is not right for Muslims to retaliate against the Jews living in other countries. Just as we deplore Islamophobia, we disapprove of Judeophobia. Historically the Jews were treated with respect in the Islamic State in Spain and elsewhere. When Muslims and Jews were expelled from Spain other Muslim States provided them both with sanctuary. Deliberating on this situation Dr. Tariq Ramadan has made the following observations. This is a condensed outline of his comments.

> Bloodshed on the land that was sanctified by the Torah, the Gospels and the Qur'ān is causing humanity to despair. Yet, any attempt to legitimise anti-Semitism on the basis of texts taken from the Islamic tradition, and as an expression of protest against the suffering of the Palestinians, must be firmly rejected. Anti-Semitic utterances have been heard from frustrated and confused young Muslims. Even knowledgeable Muslims in every crisis or political backsliding see the hand of the 'Jewish lobby'. There is nothing in Islam that gives legitimisation to Judeophobia, xenophobia and the rejection of any human being because of his religion or the group to which he belongs.

To sum up, Islam seeks to create a society where everyone is equal except in righteous achievement. In this field, Islam invites all human beings to compete and prove their moral worth. Everyone is a "pilgrim" on the road to achievement through obedience to God. It is a pity and it hurts to say that Muslims who are in possession of such a splendid and comprehensive system of life look elsewhere for guidance. It is even more painful to record that Muslim governments ignore and violate Islamic teachings while paying lip service to their religion. Unlike other systems the Islamic model was tried and tested. It worked but humanity could not protect it. Its blessings continued for more than a thousand years. It should be our endeavour to stand up and try to establish this way of life again.

Let us pray that Allah (*swt*) will guide the Muslim *Ummah* to establish that system of peace and justice in which all humanity can live in harmony.

(*Āmīn*)

Further Reading

- Abul A'lā Mawdūdī: *Human Rights in Islam*. The Islamic Foundation, 1976
- *The Universal Islamic Declaration of Human Rights*. Islamic Council of Europe, 1981
- A.K. Brohi: *Islam & Human Rights*. The UK Islamic Mission, n.d.

Animal Rights

وَٱلۡأَنۡعَٰمَ خَلَقَهَاۗ لَكُمۡ فِيهَا دِفۡءٞ وَمَنَٰفِعُ وَمِنۡهَا تَأۡكُلُونَ ﴿٥﴾
وَلَكُمۡ فِيهَا جَمَالٌ حِينَ تُرِيحُونَ وَحِينَ تَسۡرَحُونَ ﴿٦﴾ وَتَحۡمِلُ
أَثۡقَالَكُمۡ إِلَىٰ بَلَدٖ لَّمۡ تَكُونُواْ بَٰلِغِيهِ إِلَّا بِشِقِّ ٱلۡأَنفُسِۚ إِنَّ
رَبَّكُمۡ لَرَءُوفٞ رَّحِيمٞ ﴿٧﴾ وَٱلۡخَيۡلَ وَٱلۡبِغَالَ وَٱلۡحَمِيرَ لِتَرۡكَبُوهَا
وَزِينَةٗۚ وَيَخۡلُقُ مَا لَا تَعۡلَمُونَ ﴿٨﴾

And cattle He has created for you: from them you derive warmth and numerous benefits and their (meat) you eat. And you have a sense of pride and beauty in them as you drive them home in the evening, and as you lead them forth to pasture in the morning. And they carry your heavy loads to lands that you could not (otherwise) reach except with souls distressed: for your Lord is indeed most Kind, most Merciful. And (He has created) horses, mules and donkeys for you to ride and use for show; and He has created (other) things of which you have no knowledge.

(al-Naḥl 16: 5-8)

Indeed it is Allah's Mercy and Kindness that He has made provision for the human race to survive on this earth. Our lives would be deprived of many necessities without the animal kingdom. Animals provide us with meat and dairy products for our consumption. We obtain wool from them to make clothes and blankets to keep us warm. Their skins and furs yield warm raiment, rugs and bedding. Even their hairs and horns are used to make useful artefacts. We have also used them as a means of transport from time immemorial and even now we are still dependent on them. We should be thankful and grateful to Allah *(swt)*, the Provider of these amenities.

Animal rights has become a very controversial and important debate in our society. There are many philosophical, ethical and legal issues involved in this. There are also many animal rights and welfare organisations actively engaged in pressurising society and the government to accept their views. Some of the extremist organisations have even resorted to violence to force others to their viewpoint. The reason that this debate is now taking place in the West is perhaps a sense of guilt regarding its treatment of animals in the past.

The story of creation narrated in the Qur'ān is the key to the relationship of human beings with the rest of the universe. God Almighty made His intention known to angels about the creation of Adam in the following words:

وَإِذْ قَالَ رَبُّكَ لِلْمَلَٰٓئِكَةِ إِنِّي جَاعِلٌ فِي ٱلْأَرْضِ خَلِيفَةً ... ﴿٣٠﴾

Behold your Lord said to the angels: "I will create a vicegerent on earth."

(al-Baqarah 2: 30)

By this statement Muslim scholars deduce that man, as a steward, is a trustee for utilising all the earth's resources. He should not abuse or destroy them. He is required to use these resources on trust following the guidance given by God. AbdulWahid Hamid in his book *Islam the Natural Way* observed:

> This trust requires you to respect and fulfil the needs of your own body, mind and soul, as well as the needs and rights of other creation – human beings, animals and the environment as a whole.

Allah (*swt*) informs us that:

وَمَا مِن دَآبَّةٍ فِي ٱلْأَرْضِ وَلَا طَٰٓئِرٍ يَطِيرُ بِجَنَاحَيْهِ إِلَّآ أُمَمٌ أَمْثَالُكُم ... ﴿٣٨﴾

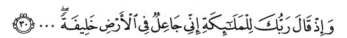

There is not an animal (that lives) on earth, nor a being that flies on its wings, but (forms part of) communities like you.
(al-An'ām 6: 38)

As such we are required to treat them with respect and use them for the purpose for which they were created. The Prophet (*ṣaws*) showed us the right way to treat animals. He told the story of a woman who would be punished because she locked up a cat without feeding it and refused to allow it to fend for itself. He commended a person who saved a dog's life by giving it water to drink. The Prophet of Islam forbade leaving animals to starve and damned a group of people who used a bird as a target. He admonished a person when he found that he had been inadequately feeding his camel and putting it to excessive work. On another occasion, he told his followers to let them graze well if the deserts are green, but travel fast if they are parched and dry, so that the animals arrive quickly at their destination and are so saved from thirst and hunger on the way. Animals should be well fed and well looked after. The blessed Prophet said:

اتَّقُوا اللَّهَ فِي هَذِهِ الْبَهَائِمِ ثُمَّ ارْكَبُوهَا صِحَاحًا

(النسائي)

Fear God in respect of these animals. Ride them when they are in good health.
(Nasā'ī)

The Qur'ān also mentions the aesthetic functions of these creatures in addition to their other utilities, sources of sustenance and transport. In the vast and beautiful variety of plant and animal life, human beings receive pleasure and enjoyment. The flora and fauna of the world contribute to man's peace of mind, a factor that is essential for his full and proper functioning.

The Glorious Qur'ān also mentions other functions that these creatures perform and which we may not perceive. They too acknowledge their Creator and glorify Him in their own God-inspired ways. Allah says:

وَإِن مِّن شَيْءٍ إِلَّا يُسَبِّحُ بِحَمْدِهِۦ وَلَٰكِن لَّا تَفْقَهُونَ تَسْبِيحَهُمْ ... ﴿٤٤﴾

There is not a thing but celebrates His praise, and yet you understand not how they declare His glory.

(al-Isrā' 17: 44)

Animal husbandry is an ancient occupation. Man has domesticated farm animals and used them for dairy products and slaughtered them for meat. Human beings need them to survive. The Animal Rights Movement is strongly opposed to this practice. Harriet Schleifer writes in a book edited by Peter Singer:

> Domestication itself is an unnatural process; it is a method of enslaving animals and subjecting their life processes to our will. Animal liberation would return domestic animals to their wild origins, free to pursue their destinies without human interference.
>
> (*In Defence of Animals*, p.72)

The absurdity of this suggestion would perhaps lead us to policing the jungle in order to save the docile cow from the hunting tiger. But how then would tigers survive? We may well also ask: do plants not possess life and feel pain? They certainly die. What right do we have to cultivate them and process them for our food? We should certainly leave them to grow in the wild without molestation. Animal rights activists seeing the absurdity of their claim concede that we have to eat them or face starvation. Thus, they do agree that human life is more precious than other life forms.

Of course we should be kind to animals. We oppose their abuse. We abhor intensive farming practices. We support those who protest about their transportation without proper care and comfort. The Islamic teachings always give the balanced view in all human affairs. The Prophet (*ṣaws*) said:

إِنَّ اللَّهَ كَتَبَ ٱلْإِحْسَانَ عَلَى كُلِّ شَيْءٍ فَإِذَا قَتَلْتُمْ فَأَحْسِنُوا الْقِتْلَةَ وَإِذَا ذَبَحْتُمْ
فَأَحْسِنُوا الذَّبْحَ وَلْيُحِدَّ أَحَدُكُمْ شَفْرَتَهُ فَلْيُرِحْ ذَبِيحَتَهُ

(مسلم)

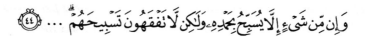

> Allah has prescribed proficiency and the most suitable way of doing everything. Do it well when you slaughter an animal. And each one of you should sharpen his knife, give comfort to the animal, slaughter it in such a way that its life departs quickly and is not left to suffer for a long time.
>
> (Muslim)

He further instructed that animals should be fed and watered before slaughter and that an animal should not be killed within sight of other animals, so sensitive was he for their feelings (Bukhārī and Muslim). Despite this humane method of slaughter voices are raised to ban Islamic and Jewish methods of slaughter and have the compulsory stunning of animals before slaughter as if this is not equally painful for animals.

Hunting for food is allowed, as this may be the only way to survive for those who are travelling or living in isolated places. Fishing is another method of obtaining food from the sea, which again is a target by the latest campaign of the Vegetarian Society called Suffering Seas! But to hunt for pleasure and to kill for fun is an obnoxious sport and it is made completely unlawful in Islam. The Prophet (*ṣaws*) forbade shooting arrows at any cattle or bird which was tied or held up. He banned hitting or branding an animal on its face. He ordered the chicks to be released. He said:

مَنْ قَتَلَ عُصْفُورًا فَمَا فَوْقَهَا بِغَيْرِ حَقِّهَا سَأَلَهُ اللَّهُ عَزَّ وَجَلَّ عَنْهَا يَوْمَ الْقِيَامَةِ

(أحمد)

> A person will be answerable before God on the Day of Judgement for unjustly killing a sparrow or even a smaller bird.
>
> (Aḥmad)

He once found someone who had burned an ants' nest. He told him that the prerogative of punishment with fire belonged only to God. He forbade setting animals to fight against each other. He encouraged acts of kindness to animals. Thus Islam teaches and lays great stress on kindness, mercy and care for animals, but equally allows man to use them for human needs.

The other area of concern is experiments on living animals. It is estimated that millions of animals die in laboratories around the world every year. The worrying aspect of these experiments on living animals is that significant numbers are performed without the use of anaesthesia as if they were minor experiments. Experiments also involve the deliberate induction of psychological stress. Some experiments involve burning and scalding or exposure to ionising irradiation. There is a heated debate going on between biomedical scientists and anti-vivisectionists. Those who support the research accuse the others of not caring for human misery and suffering. They claim that vaccinations and other drugs which bring relief to the incurably ill must continue to be produced using animals as "guinea pigs". The Islamic view on this is to scrutinise the need for experimentation and to stop all unnecessary experiments in which animals die or are put under stress. The research community should try to find alternatives to helpless animals and should be required to work under very strict guidelines.

The tactics adopted by the Animal Liberation Front of sending letter bombs or placing bombs in laboratories to maim or kill people and cause mayhem are equally reprehensible. The reason they put forward to justify their action is that only such actions will bring this issue to the political level and achieve results. The same argument is used to protest against exporting live animals: it attracts attention to their cause; it stretches the resources of the community and becomes very expensive to police and will eventually lead to a stoppage of the export trade. It is expected that those who care so much about animals should also be concerned about their own species. There are thousands of women and children dying in Palestine, Iraq, Bosnia, Rwanda, Chechnya and other parts of the world. The misery of human beings should also touch their hearts and they should also protest about their plight.

We have touched on various issues we face in our interaction with animals. We have to strike the right balance. There are those who worship animals. There are those who walk bare-foot and do not use shoes because they are made of leather, some even put a thin cloth over their mouth and nose to avoid breathing in any moth. There are vegetarians and those who do not eat eggs or fish. Then there are others who kill animals for sport and game. There are others who perform cruel experiments on animals and kill them. There are those who have factory farms in which animals can hardly move and where chickens are bred and fed in confined spaces and do not see the light of day. There are others who trade in exotic animals for the pet industry yet half of these animals die in transit. There are still those who export live animals in the most cramped conditions without adequate food or water and with the sole aim of maximising their profits.

Among all these variations we have to find ways of treating animals which involve neither veneration nor exploitation. It is only God, Who has created both human beings and animals that can guide us to what our proper relationship should be. Islam gives moral values as well as practical advice based on mercy, justice and moderation in all our affairs. We hope all those who are perturbed by what is happening in our society will think seriously about the guidance provided by Islam in this respect and develop caring and balanced attitudes, policies and behaviour in all our affairs.

Let us pray that we follow the guidance Allah (*swt*) has given us in treating our dumb friends with kindness and compassion.

(*Āmīn*)

Further Reading

- Peter Singer (ed.): *In Defence of Animals*. Oxford: Blackwell, 1985
- Robert Garner: *Animals, Politics and Morality*. Manchester University Press, 1993
- Ghulam Mustafa Khan: *Al-Zabah: slaying animals for food, the Islamic way*. Green Link, n.d.
- Basheer Ahmad Masri: *Islamic concern for animals*. Athene Trust, n.d.

Care of the Environment

ٱلرَّحۡمَٰنُ ﴿١﴾ عَلَّمَ ٱلۡقُرۡءَانَ ﴿٢﴾ خَلَقَ ٱلۡإِنسَٰنَ ﴿٣﴾ عَلَّمَهُ ٱلۡبَيَانَ ﴿٤﴾
ٱلشَّمۡسُ وَٱلۡقَمَرُ بِحُسۡبَانٖ ﴿٥﴾ وَٱلنَّجۡمُ وَٱلشَّجَرُ يَسۡجُدَانِ ﴿٦﴾ وَٱلسَّمَآءَ
رَفَعَهَا وَوَضَعَ ٱلۡمِيزَانَ ﴿٧﴾ أَلَّا تَطۡغَوۡاْ فِي ٱلۡمِيزَانِ ﴿٨﴾ وَأَقِيمُواْ
ٱلۡوَزۡنَ بِٱلۡقِسۡطِ وَلَا تُخۡسِرُواْ ٱلۡمِيزَانَ ﴿٩﴾

(Allah) Most Gracious! It is He Who has taught the Qur'ān. He has created man. He has taught him speech. The sun and the moon follow courses (exactly) computed; and the stars and the trees – both (alike) bow in adoration. And the Firmament has He raised high, and He has set up the Balance (of Justice), in order that you may not transgress (due) balance. So establish weight with justice and fall not short in the balance.

(al-Raḥmān 55: 1-9)

Environmental issues have been on the agenda of most developing and developed nations. They have also been discussed at many international conferences and were the subject of a Convention at the Earth Summit in Rio in 1992. Most predictions about the state of our planet are depressing: essentially the human race continues to destroy the world's ecosystem in its quest for industrial progress and prosperity. It is predicted that if we do not take drastic action and cut back our profligate resource use 40 percent of the world's remaining forests will disappear and with them 20 percent of species are likely to become extinct. As a consequence of global environmental pollution and deforestation there is an increase in carbon dioxide build-up, a depletion of ozone levels, a spread of hazardous wastes and increase in acid rains. As a result of industrialisation and the emission of greenhouse gases, global temperatures are rising, which is causing violent weather conditions around the world. Already El Nino – the vast, climatic phenomenon that carries warm surface waters from the west to the east Pacific – is devastating fisheries and bringing storms and drought. This now happens every two years, as opposed to every six years. To combat this world catastrophe the Kyoto Agreement of December 1997 allocated emissions quotas to the various developed countries, as they are more responsible for the cause of pollution. Sadly the United States and some other countries have refused to sign this international agreement. Thus, the world is still sitting on a time bomb.

As Muslims we should regard care of the environment as our sacred duty. Allah (*swt*) gave this responsibility to humanity when He appointed the Prophet Adam (peace be upon him), the first human being, as *Khalīfah*. This means that he was honoured as a vicegerent and steward of the earth and its resources. In the Qur'ān this responsibility is called *al-amānah* – the trust. As a trustee each one of us is duty-bound to use the resources of the earth as well as to preserve them and leave them in better shape for succeeding generations. We should not waste them nor destroy and deplete them. Mankind has a special place in Allah's scheme of creation. We are not just friends of the earth we are also its guardians. Just as Allah sustains and cares for the world we as His vicegerents must nurture and care for the earth and its environment. We will betray the trust (*al-amānah*) if we neglect such proper care of the natural world.

So what are the Islamic teachings about preserving the environment? First, we are prohibited from polluting it. One of the most important and basic Islamic teachings is *ṭahārah* (purification) and *naẓāfah* (cleanliness). We have to stay in a state of purity for performing our prayers. The main purpose of this apart from worshipping our Creator is *tazkiyah,* which means purification. Of course cleanliness and purification are opposed to pollution and corruption. Thus, Islam wants Muslims to be pure physically as well as morally. There is a well-known *ḥadīth* of the Prophet (*ṣaws*) that states: "Purity is half of faith." (Muslim) This *ḥadīth* signifies the importance of purification in our lives.

Second, we have to lead a balanced life and avoid excesses. This is true both in our behaviour and our use of resources. Allah in *Sūrah al-Raḥmān* asks us not to transgress but establish balance and justice in our dealings with others. Addressing mankind He says:

يَٰبَنِيٓ ءَادَمَ خُذُواْ زِينَتَكُمۡ عِندَ كُلِّ مَسۡجِدٖ وَكُلُواْ وَٱشۡرَبُواْ وَلَا تُسۡرِفُوٓاْۚ
إِنَّهُۥ لَا يُحِبُّ ٱلۡمُسۡرِفِينَ ٣١

O children of Adam! Wear your beautiful apparel at every time and place of worship: eat and drink: but waste not by excess, for Allah loves not the wasters.

(al-Aʿrāf 7: 31)

If we waste and deplete the resources of the earth we create an imbalance in nature and problems for ourselves and also for the rest of Allah's creation. Just as increases in greenhouse gases and depletion of the ozone layer has resulted in disastrous climatic changes. Allah (*swt*) draws our attention to what may occur if human beings, indifferent to the various types of balances, go too far in exploiting the environment, which is what we are witnessing today. He says:

ظَهَرَ ٱلۡفَسَادُ فِي ٱلۡبَرِّ وَٱلۡبَحۡرِ بِمَا كَسَبَتۡ أَيۡدِي ٱلنَّاسِ ... ٤١

Corruption has prevailed on land and sea because of what man's hands have earned...

(al-Rūm 30: 41)

He also says:

وَلَوۡ بَسَطَ ٱللَّهُ ٱلرِّزۡقَ لِعِبَادِهِۦ لَبَغَوۡاْ فِي ٱلۡأَرۡضِ ... ٢٧

If Allah were to bestow abundance upon His servants, they would behave on the earth with wanton insolence.

(al-Shūrā 42: 27)

The problem is not that human beings should not exploit the resources of the earth for these have been created for us to use. And in order to develop and progress we need natural resources. The problem rather lies in extravagance, transgression and extremism. This leads to distortion of the fine balance and thus upsets natural stability. This corrupts the environment and natural habitat for humans and other species. Allah ordains:

كُلُوا۟ وَٱشْرَبُوا۟ مِن رِّزْقِ ٱللَّهِ وَلَا تَعْثَوْا۟ فِى ٱلْأَرْضِ مُفْسِدِينَ ﴿٦٠﴾

Eat and drink of the sustenance God has provided,
and do not corrupt the earth with evil.

(al-Baqarah 2: 60)

Allah's prophets have also repeatedly warned their people to refrain from corrupting the earth with evil.

To safeguard the environment and our heritage, our first duty is to practise moderation in all our affairs. To waste and lavishly squander is a criminal act and it is being ungrateful to Allah. In *Sūrah al-Isrā'* it is said:

وَلَا تُبَذِّرْ تَبْذِيرًا ﴿٢٦﴾ إِنَّ ٱلْمُبَذِّرِينَ كَانُوٓا۟ إِخْوَٰنَ ٱلشَّيَٰطِينِ ۖ
وَكَانَ ٱلشَّيْطَٰنُ لِرَبِّهِۦ كَفُورًا ﴿٢٧﴾

Squander not in the manner of a spendthrift. Verily
spendthrifts are brothers of Satan; and Satan is
to his Lord ungrateful.

(al-Isrā' 17: 26-27)

Despite this specific injunction an enormous amount of wealth is squandered in sumptuous wedding feasts and ostentatious decorations. The other type of corruption the human race is guilty of is uprooting vegetation and animals. Allah draws our attention to this as well:

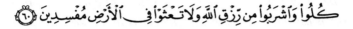

وَمِنَ ٱلنَّاسِ مَن يُعْجِبُكَ قَوْلُهُۥ فِى ٱلْحَيَوٰةِ ٱلدُّنْيَا وَيُشْهِدُ ٱللَّهَ عَلَىٰ مَا فِى
قَلْبِهِۦ وَهُوَ أَلَدُّ ٱلْخِصَامِ ﴿٢٠٤﴾ وَإِذَا تَوَلَّىٰ سَعَىٰ فِى ٱلْأَرْضِ لِيُفْسِدَ فِيهَا
وَيُهْلِكَ ٱلْحَرْثَ وَٱلنَّسْلَ ۗ وَٱللَّهُ لَا يُحِبُّ ٱلْفَسَادَ ﴿٢٠٥﴾

There is a type of person whose speech about this world's life may dazzle you, and he calls Allah to witness about what is in his heart; yet he is the most contentious of enemies. When he turns his back, his aim everywhere is to spread corruption through the earth and destroy crops and cattle. Allah does not like corruption.

(al-Baqarah 2: 204-205)

Surely this flagrant exploitation of the environment and habitat without any check or control is a gross injustice. It is nothing less than being ungrateful for the favours our Creator has bestowed upon us. This is betraying the trust and disregarding the responsibility of the stewardship given to us. We are required to look after our natural resources and safeguard them for future generations. This is explained in a parable by Allah:

قَرْيَةً كَانَتْ ءَامِنَةً مُّطْمَئِنَّةً يَأْتِيهَا رِزْقُهَا رَغَدًا مِّن كُلِّ
مَكَانٍ فَكَفَرَتْ بِأَنْعُمِ ٱللَّهِ فَأَذَٰقَهَا ٱللَّهُ لِبَاسَ ٱلْجُوعِ
وَٱلْخَوْفِ بِمَا كَانُوا۟ يَصْنَعُونَ ﴿١١٢﴾

A city enjoying security and quiet, abundantly supplied with sustenance from every place. But it was ungrateful for Allah's favours. Therefore, He inflicted it with famine and terror (in extremes) (closing in on it) like a garment (from every side), because of the (evil) which (its people) committed.

(al-Nahl 16: 112)

In order to put into practice Islamic teachings on care for the environment, the Prophet (*ṣaws*) and his Companions set an example to be followed by succeeding generations. To encourage vegetation and enhance a benevolent environment the Prophet (*ṣaws*) said:

> Whenever a Muslim plants or grows a sapling or a plant, and a human being, a beast or anything else feeds upon it, it is counted for him as an act of *ṣadaqah* (benevolence).
>
> (Muslim)

The Prophet (*ṣaws*) was the pioneer in establishing a conservation area, where trees could not be cut down and animals could not be killed. Allah's Messenger protected the whole of Madinah, section by section, where no tree could be uprooted and nothing bigger than what could be used to drive a camel could be cut (Abū Dā'ūd). He said about the city that:

إِنِّي أُحَرِّمُ مَا بَيْنَ لاَبَتَي الْمَدِينَةِ أَنْ يُقْطَعَ عِضَاهُهَا أَوْ يُقْتَلَ صَيْدُهَا

(مسلم)

> I forbid the trees between the two lavas of Madinah to be cut down and the game to be killed.
>
> (Muslim)

To keep the environment clean and preserve the purity of water resources his injunction included:

عَنْ جَابِرٍ عَنْ رَسُولِ اللَّهِ صَلَّى اللَّهُ عَلَيْهِ وَسَلَّمَ أَنَّهُ نَهَى
أَنْ يُبَالَ فِي الْمَاءِ الرَّاكِدِ

(ابن ماجة)

> Let no one urinate in stagnant water.
>
> (Ibn Mājah)

and

اتَّقُوا الْمَلاَعِنَ الثَّلاَثَةَ الْبَرَازَ فِي الْمَوَارِدِ وَقَارِعَةِ الطَّرِيقِ وَالظِّلِّ

(أبو داود)

Avoid the three actions that bring people's curses: defecating in water sources, on roads and in the shade.
(Abū Dā'ūd)

It is our duty to implement the guidance given by Allah and His Prophet individually and collectively. We should be vigilant and guard our environment and censure its corruption. Allah says:

فَلَوْلَا كَانَ مِنَ ٱلْقُرُونِ مِن قَبْلِكُمْ أُوْلُوا۟ بَقِيَّةٍ يَنْهَوْنَ عَنِ ٱلْفَسَادِ فِى ٱلْأَرْضِ ... ﴿١١٦﴾

Why were there not among the generations before you some upright persons prohibiting corruption on earth?
(Hūd 11: 116)

Let us remind ourselves that we are the trustees of this earth and all its resources and that it is our duty to maintain a clean and pure environment and block all sources of defilement and corruption. May Allah, Almighty help us in this resolve.

(*Āmīn*)

Further Reading

- Fazlun Khalid and Joanne O'Brien (eds.): *Islam and Ecology*. Cassell, 1992
- M.H. Khayat: *Environmental Health: an Islamic Perspective*. Alexandria: World Health Organisation, 1997
- Mawil Izzi Din: *The Environmental Dimensions of Islam*. Cambridge: Lutterworth Press, 2000
- Robin Attfield: *The Ethics of the Global Environment*. Edinburgh University Press, 1999

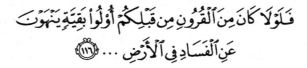

Muslims in the West

ٱدْعُ إِلَىٰ سَبِيلِ رَبِّكَ بِٱلْحِكْمَةِ وَٱلْمَوْعِظَةِ ٱلْحَسَنَةِ ۖ وَجَٰدِلْهُم
بِٱلَّتِى هِىَ أَحْسَنُ ۚ إِنَّ رَبَّكَ هُوَ أَعْلَمُ بِمَن ضَلَّ عَن سَبِيلِهِۦ ۖ
وَهُوَ أَعْلَمُ بِٱلْمُهْتَدِينَ ﴿١٢٥﴾

Invite (all) to the way of your Lord with wisdom and beautiful preaching; and argue with them in ways that are best and most gracious: for your Lord knows best who have strayed from His path and who receive guidance.
(al-Naḥl 16: 125)

The Muslims have been in Europe over a long period of history. They ruled Spain for more than 700 years (711-1492) but were finally defeated and totally eliminated. They were in Sicily for 260 years (831-1091) yet their fate was no different from that in Spain. The Ottoman Turks were in Eastern Europe – they camped on the banks of the River Danube and knocked on the doors of Vienna – but they too shrank back. It is only now that many millions of Muslims have made Europe their home. After Christianity, Islam is the second largest faith in many European countries. Europe has a very long association with the Muslim world. This stretches back to the times of the Crusades followed by trade links with the Middle East, India and the Far East. Then from the eighteenth century onwards many European countries were imperial powers dominating the Muslim world. Despite these long historical and current encounters between Islam and the West, there is still a certain degree of ignorance and misunderstanding about Islam and Muslims. Portrayals of Islam in the Western media have continued to perpetuate the stereotyped image of Muslims.

In earlier encounters, Muslims came and dominated European lands. Their rule was paramount and they dealt from a position of strength. Today, the Muslim world is in disarray. The Muslims seem to be defeated intellectually, politically and socially. They are divided and disintegrated, feeling low, weak, uncertain, humiliated and overawed by the forces of the West. This time they have come to the West to acquire education as the Muslim world lags behind in science and technology. Some have come seeking employment or asylum as they see little prospect of living in peace in their own lands. Thus, Muslims are in a weak and vulnerable situation in the West.

When I reflect on this situation I think there must be some *ḥikmah* (wisdom) behind all this. Allah (*swt*) brought us here to acquire knowledge and insight into Western ways of life whether good or bad so that we can then successfully present Islamic *da'wah* here.

The greatest challenge Muslims face today is to win the hearts and minds of the people. It is not a war for territory. It is a war of ideology. So how can we win the hearts of others? The Prophet ʿĪsā (peace be upon him) invited his apostles, who were mainly fishermen, by saying to them "Come I will teach you how to fish men". This was the task of all prophets who wanted to save mankind from their doom. Thus, the methodology is the same as people down the centuries are the same.

First, we should realise that every human being can change. Evil can be changed into good. The Holy Qur'ān says:

وَلَا تَسْتَوِى ٱلْحَسَنَةُ وَلَا ٱلسَّيِّئَةُ ۚ ٱدْفَعْ بِٱلَّتِى هِىَ أَحْسَنُ فَإِذَا
ٱلَّذِى بَيْنَكَ وَبَيْنَهُۥ عَدَٰوَةٌ كَأَنَّهُۥ وَلِىٌّ حَمِيمٌ ﴿٣٤﴾

Goodness and Evil cannot be equal. Repel (Evil) with what is better then will he between whom and you was hatred become as it were your friend and intimate.

(Fuṣṣilat 41: 34)

So many who were bitter enemies became bosom friends. The Tartars came and destroyed the ʿAbbāsid *Khilāfah*, but they embraced Islam and then became its champions.

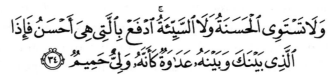

Second, every human being has been created and moulded by God Himself. Allah (*swt*) says:

فَإِذَا سَوَّيْتُهُۥ وَنَفَخْتُ فِيهِ مِن رُّوحِى ... ﴿٢٩﴾

I have fashioned him (in due proportion) and breathed into him of My Spirit.

(al-Ḥijr 15: 29)

Why should we deprive anyone of the blessings of Islam? It is the duty of the Muslim *Ummah* to approach each and everyone wherever they live. Whatever means we have we should use to inform our friends, relations, neighbours, near or far, of the blessings of the Divine Message.

Third, the key to human beings is through their hearts. 'Alī ibn Abī Ṭālib (may Allah be pleased with him) said:

> In human hearts there are some desires and inclinations. There are times when hearts are attuned to listen and at times they are not prepared for this. Hence enter their hearts through their inclinations and approach them when they are inclined to listen. As hearts go blind when they are forced (and you cannot penetrate them).
>
> (Abū Yūsuf, *Kitāb al-Kharāj*)

This explains the advice given by Allah: "Invite (people) to the way of your Lord with *ḥikmah* (wisdom) and beautiful preaching and argue with them in the ways that are best and most gracious." (al-Naḥl 16: 125)

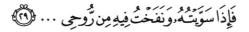

Fourth, few people are influenced by reading books or listening to speeches. Actions and noble and personal character and behaviour speak louder than words. It was the behaviour and gentle manner of the Prophet and his radiant personality and noble character that won the hearts of those who met him or talked to him. It was the dealings of our forefathers who went to the Malabar Coast of Western India, Malaysia and Indonesia as traders and spread the teachings of Islam, which converted whole nations where no Muslim army ever marched. We have to win people's hearts in the West. We have to attract them towards Islam rather then create hostility. For this we have to engage in interfaith dialogue and concentrate on building bridges of understanding. Even if we cannot bring a large number of people into the Islamic fold we can nevertheless find people like Abū Ṭālib who can support and back Islam. If we launch our campaign in this way it is quite possible that we will have Allah's help and eventually the atmosphere of hatred towards Islam will dissolve. If authentic Islamic teachings reach the masses it is bound to captivate their hearts.

Five, instead of resorting to violence, extremism and emotionalism we have to adopt a judicious approach to capture the hearts of our audience. If such slogans are raised that frighten them or cause offence then why should they listen to us? On the contrary if we approach them with sagacity and engage ourselves for the welfare of society then the masses of these countries will become our valuable asset. It is vital for the people of the West to understand the religion and culture of Muslims and it is equally vital for Muslims to appreciate Western values of democracy, fair dealing and equity.

Six, a serious challenge faced by the Muslim *Ummah* is to achieve intellectual superiority. We should be putting forward solutions to solve the problems of modern times. We have to make inroads in this society and make the doubts and suspicions raised about Islam and the *Sharī'ah* ineffective.

Seven, in Western countries where there is a democratic tradition, power is not exclusively in the domain of central government. Popularly elected members belonging to opposition parties, local councillors, representatives of the media, pressure groups, central and local government bureaucracy, all have some influence in shaping government policies and decisions. If by our presence we influence them then our point of view and our message can reach the corridors of power.

Muslims are now neighbours with non-Muslims, we are part of the European labour force and our children are growing up within a multi-cultural and multi-religious society. We form a part of European life. Thus, we should live in complete harmony with each other instead of through doubt and mistrust. As Muslims we should share our beliefs with our neighbours and fellow human beings. Muslims living as minority in a non-Muslim state have a great opportunity to convey the message of Islam through their character and moral behaviour.

Let us pray that Allah (*swt*) may guide us to realise our responsibility and give us courage to perform our duties and thus make our society peaceful and harmonious.

(*Āmīn*)

Further Reading

- Syed Abul Hasan 'Alī Nadvī: *Muslims in the West.* Leicester: The Islamic Foundation, 1983
- Isma'īl. R. Faruqī: *The Path of Da'wah in the West.* London: The UK Islamic Mission, 1986

Integration

وَمِنْ ءَايَـٰتِهِۦ خَلْقُ ٱلسَّمَـٰوَٰتِ وَٱلْأَرْضِ وَٱخْتِلَـٰفُ أَلْسِنَتِكُمْ
وَأَلْوَٰنِكُمْ إِنَّ فِى ذَٰلِكَ لَـَٔايَـٰتٍ لِّلْعَـٰلِمِينَ ﴿٢٢﴾

And among His Signs is the creation of the heavens and the earth, and the variations in your languages and your colours; verily in that are signs for those who know.
(al-Rūm 30: 22)

Muslims in Britain have come from different parts of the Muslim world. They have come with some specific purpose, either to acquire education and skills, or to obtain better employment or to seek asylum from oppressive regimes. Many came with the intention of staying here for a short period of time only to return back home. But a large majority stayed behind and brought their families to settle here. Now there is a new generation of Muslims who have been born and educated in Britain. These Muslims together with other communities are now part of a multi-faith and multi-cultural British society. However, their presence in a non-Muslim country raises many problems for Muslims. They have come from a significantly different cultural and religious background. The problem of settling in a very different cultural environment has yet to be solved.

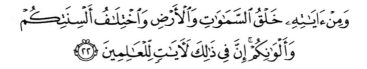

Initially, when the Muslims were exposed to different social values and cultures their instinctive reaction was to safeguard their own values and cultures. This initial reaction to remain in isolation, shutting themselves off from the rest of society in order to preserve their Islamic identity still persists. Some still manage to remain in this state. We know the futility of such an inward-looking attitude. One cannot preserve one's identity by shutting oneself off from the rest of the world. Such isolationism has come under severe criticism both from official agencies and many Muslim organisations as well. This because non-cooperation and non-communication is detrimental to both the individual and society at large.

There is another group among the Muslims that wants to assimilate completely with Western values and culture by abandoning Islamic teachings. Such people are also to be found in many Muslim countries. They are dazzled by the progress and material prosperity of the West and they think that by adopting Western ways this will help Muslim countries to modernise and prosper. However such blind imitation and aping will not help change the destiny of Muslim nations. We have the recent example of Turkey that tried to adopt Western laws and norms yet it was not able to modernise and prosper. Such capitulation of our values and culture is both irrational and disrespectful of our identity.

In the last few years there is a new phenomena of extremism has emerged in our midst. A small vociferous group advocates confrontation with the West. It wants to destroy Western norms and values and wants to replace them by Islamic values. This extremism, of course, has no sanction in the Islamic *Sharīʿah*. All prophets conveyed the message of peace and harmony. They wanted to reform society from within and did not enforce their views by violent means. They even endured the violence committed against them without retaliation. To adopt such an attitude is both dangerous and counter-productive.

So what is the alternative to these three extremes? We know that Islam wants people to be involved in the affairs of their community. We have been advised to follow the precept of Islam that is 'to accept what is good and reject what is wrong'. It is our duty to understand and evaluate Western culture. This does not entail outright rejection nor does it require complete absorption. We have to analyse all aspects of Western culture and decide what similarities and what differences it has as compared with our own culture. Then we should decide what is desirable and what is not.

In saying that we have to adopt independent critical appreciation and assume that we have an ideological and cultural personality of our own. This ideological and cultural personality is embodied in the basic guidance given by Allah (*swt*) and His Prophet (*ṣaws*). This guidance teaches us to be conscious at all times of our commitment to our faith.

One cannot form any relationship with society if one is not clear about one's own relationship with one's Creator. In Islam, Allah is our Creator, the Lord, the Nourisher and the Law Giver. The position of man is that he is God's representative on this earth. He has to live his life according to Allah's guidance. This relationship with Allah fosters our integration with the universe and with reality. Problems of alienation then are the result of not fully understanding the reality of ourselves and of the universe. Once a person establishes the right relationship with his Creator he integrates with reality and also with his own self.

Our relationship with Allah also fosters our meaningful relations with society. The Prophet (*ṣaws*) enunciated this guiding principle as follows: *"Al-Dīn* is *naṣīḥah"*. The people asked "To whom?" The Prophet replied, "To Allah and His Book and to His Messenger and the leaders of the Muslims and their common folk." (Muslim)

Naṣīḥah is difficult to translate into English. It embraces sincerity, good advice and well-wishing. The word has two meanings. One meaning is to clean, to purify or to improve something such as purifying honey from impurities and the other meaning is to unite or to join something together such as when sewing a garment. In the Holy Qur'ān this word is used to describe the task which the Prophets have performed in respect of their *Ummah*.

فَتَوَلَّىٰ عَنْهُمْ وَقَالَ يَٰقَوْمِ لَقَدْ أَبْلَغْتُكُمْ رِسَالَةَ رَبِّي وَنَصَحْتُ
لَكُمْ وَلَٰكِن لَّا تُحِبُّونَ ٱلنَّٰصِحِينَ ﴿٧٩﴾

So Ṣāliḥ left them, saying: "O my people! I did indeed convey to you the message for which I was sent by my Lord. I gave you good counsel, but you love not good counsellors."

(al-Aʿrāf 7: 79)

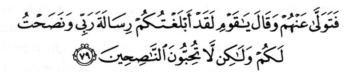

Naṣīḥah signifies sincere relationship with society. It is a heartfelt desire to reform and to build relationships on the right lines as well as wishing for the well-being of the whole community. So *naṣīḥah* is a dynamic and purposeful activity. It involves a Muslim with his surroundings. In this *ḥadīth*, *naṣīḥah* in respect of Allah means absolute sincerity and devotion to Him and that we establish correct relations with Him. *Naṣīḥah* in respect of the Prophet is to accept him as the supreme guide and leader. And *naṣīḥah* in respect of the leaders of the Muslim society and common folk is basically to give them good advice, that is enjoining what is good and forbidding what is wrong. Thus, a Muslim's life is to be sincere to oneself and to the rest of society.

With this duty of *naṣīḥah* as our motivating force we should embark upon critical analysis and deep thought. When we are confronted with a different culture and environment we should ask questions such as: "Is it right to follow this custom?" "Is this Islamically acceptable behaviour?" or "Should we pursue this course of action?" Thus, we have to make conscious decisions on each issue and adopt our course of action accordingly. Looking at some aspects of the West we can see that there are some institutions and features of British society like its democratic traditions, equality, honesty, fair dealing, punctuality and good manners, helping others, etc. that we can say are also Islamic values and that Muslims should follow them. We should willingly adopt all good things wherever we find them. But then there are other things also prevalent in British society such as sexual permissiveness, one-parent families, old peoples' homes, pornography and hooliganism. Muslims cannot adopt these aspects of British culture, as we know they are detrimental for society and also violate Islamic teachings. This should be the general attitude of Muslims living in Britain and other Western countries.

No doubt there is a group among the Muslims who prefer to live in isolation so as to preserve their identity. But they are in the minority and they have to be persuaded to come out of their self-imposed shell and get involved in the task of reforming society and making it better for everyone. An individual can still retain his identity in integration. This is different from assimilation whereby one is completely absorbed into and thus loses one's identity.

The other important task that we have to do is to get rid of the baggage of some cultural traditions that are not Islamic, for example forcing our offspring to marry against their will. This because forced marriages are void under Islamic law. Yet there are many reported cases of such incidents. This tarnishes the image of Islam in this country. But arranged marriages that are prevalent in other cultures as well are of course different from forced marriages. The treatment of women by some sections of Muslim society is clearly against Islamic teachings. In Islam, women have equal rights in pursuing education and contributing to the welfare of their families and society. They should not be left uneducated, ignorant and confined to their homes.

Historically, Islam has tried to assimilate the local culture when it is not in conflict with Islamic teachings. Right from Indonesia to Morocco there is diversity of culture despite all being Muslim countries. In time there will be a European and British Islamic culture.

Muslims who have now made Britain their home are exposed to many challenges and hurdles. These can only be met by being conscious of our ideological and cultural heritage. We can meet this challenge and check the onslaught of Western culture by adopting Islamic values ourselves and by seeing that our houses are in order. By following the precept of *naṣīḥah* we will then be safeguarding our society. We should acquire those skills and capabilities so that we can meet the challenges of our age.

Let us pray that Allah (*swt*) may give us this wisdom to discern between good and evil and guide us to the right path.

(*Āmīn*)

Further Reading

- Tariq Ramadan: *To Be a European Muslim*. Markfield: The Islamic Foundation, 1999
- Mohamed Fathi Osman: *The Children of Adam: an Islamic Perspective on Pluralism*. Washington, DC: Georgetown University, 1997
- Abdur Rehman Momin: 'Pluralism and Multiculturalism: an Islamic Perspective'. *American Journal of Islamic Social Sciences,* Vol. 18 (2), Spring 2001, pp. 115-146
- Ataullah Siddiqui: 'Believing and Belonging in a Pluralistic Society'. In: David A. Hart, *Multi-Faith Britain*. Alresford, Hants.: O Books, 2002

Our Relationship with Non-Muslims

لِكُلٍّ جَعَلْنَا مِنكُمْ شِرْعَةً وَمِنْهَاجًا ۚ وَلَوْ شَاءَ اللَّهُ لَجَعَلَكُمْ أُمَّةً
وَاحِدَةً وَلَٰكِن لِّيَبْلُوَكُمْ فِي مَا آتَاكُمْ ۖ فَاسْتَبِقُوا الْخَيْرَاتِ ۚ إِلَى اللَّهِ
مَرْجِعُكُمْ جَمِيعًا فَيُنَبِّئُكُم بِمَا كُنتُمْ فِيهِ تَخْتَلِفُونَ ﴿٤٨﴾

To each among you We have prescribed a Law and an Open Way. If Allah had so willed, He would have made you a single people, but (His plan is) to test you: so strive in a race in all virtues. The goal of all of you is to Allah; it is He that will show you the truth of the matter in which you dispute.

(al-Mā'idah 5: 48)

This is the first time in history that such a large number of Muslims reside among non-Muslims. Some are in these lands for a short time to acquire higher education or conduct business, but the vast majority have come here for economic reasons or asylum. Now they have made these countries their permanent homes. There are many implications about their stay here from the point of view of the *Sharī'ah*. Many classical *fuqahā'* (jurists) disapproved of Muslims' living for long periods of time in countries which are termed *dār al-kufr* (abode of *kufr*). The reason for their opinion was that Muslims may not be able to practise their religion in complete freedom and thus have to compromise their Islamic duties. However, now many contemporary jurists looking at the situation afresh consider these countries as *dār al-'ahd* where a Muslim may live in contractual obligations with the state. It can also be considered as *dār al-amn* (abode of peace) or *dār al-daʿwah* (abode of *daʿwah*) in which Muslims can live peacefully and fulfil their religious obligations as well as engage in *daʿwah* work among their local communities. With these intentions their stay here is permissible. If you accept this second opinion then it is your duty to integrate with society and present Islamic teachings to our host community.

Daʿwah may not be the prime reason for those who have migrated but since they have chosen to live here they might as well make it worthwhile by doing *daʿwah* work. Thus, we should develop a rapport with our hosts. They should be informed about our beliefs and practices. We have to try and dispel the ignorance and prejudice that is so prevalent about Islam and Muslims. Thus we have to be forthcoming and reach out to society. If we were to remain in isolation and concentrate ourselves in ghettos we would only perpetuate a tainted image of ourselves and be unable to illuminate the light of Islam in their homes and hearts.

Apart from our *daʿwah* obligation, what other duties do we owe this society? As we have made this country our home and the government has given us permission to stay we have entered into a binding contract to live here peacefully and to contribute to the well-being of society. We have to abide by the laws of this country. We may not approve of all its laws, yet we cannot wilfully violate them. Living in a democratic country we can lobby for changes to such laws. There may even be a few laws and regulations which interfere with the performance of our religious duties. These have to be sorted out with tact and sagacity.

We should live in this country as good citizens and should not abuse the privilege of staying here. Our non-Muslim neighbours should feel secure and safe and that they have no cause for concern because of our presence. The Prophet (*ṣaws*) said: "By God he is not a true believer, from whose mischief his neighbours do not feel secure" (Bukhārī and Muslim). We should be actively involved in preserving the peace and quiet of our neighbourhood. We should be participating in such social and cultural activities that do not conflict with Islamic teachings. There are *aḥādīth* which provide guidance about our relations with our neighbours. These are applicable to Muslims as well as people of other faiths. For example, if we cook some special dish we should share this with our neighbours. Once when ʿAbdullāh ibn ʿUmar slaughtered a goat he asked that some of its meat should be shared with his Jewish neighbour. He narrated that the Prophet (*ṣaws*) encouraged us to have good relations with our neighbours. The Prophet (*ṣaws*) is also reported to have said that Jibrīl constantly reminded him about the rights of neighbours so much so that he felt that neighbours might be included as heirs in the inheritance. There are many *aḥādīth* outlining the duties towards neighbours. These are applicable to both Muslims and non-Muslims alike. For example, greeting them, exchanging gifts, sharing food, looking after the sick and attending funerals are all part of the Prophet's teachings. Helping them in need and spending money on them come under the definition of *ṣadaqah* (benevolent acts for which there is a reward from Allah).

According to Islamic teachings, spending in the way of Allah (*infāq fī sabīl Allāh*) should not be restricted to Muslims only. Help and welfare to all human beings, whatever their faith, is the duty of believers. In *Sūrah al-Baqarah* there are extensive passages encouraging Muslims to spend their wealth on the welfare of the needy and disadvantaged members of society. In the midst of these instructions there is also this verse:

لَّيْسَ عَلَيْكَ هُدَىٰهُمْ وَلَٰكِنَّ ٱللَّهَ يَهْدِى مَن يَشَآءُ ۗ وَمَا تُنفِقُوا۟
مِنْ خَيْرٍ فَلِأَنفُسِكُمْ ۚ وَمَا تُنفِقُونَ إِلَّا ٱبْتِغَآءَ وَجْهِ ٱللَّهِ ۚ
وَمَا تُنفِقُوا۟ مِنْ خَيْرٍ يُوَفَّ إِلَيْكُمْ وَأَنتُمْ لَا تُظْلَمُونَ ﴿٢٧٢﴾

It is not required of you (O Messenger), to set them on the right path, but Allah sets on the right path whom He pleases. Whatever of good you give benefits your souls, and you shall only do so seeking the pleasure of Allah. Whatever good you give, shall be rendered back to you, and you shall not be dealt with unjustly.

(al-Baqarah 2: 272)

Mawlānā Mawdūdī in his commentary explains this verse as follows:

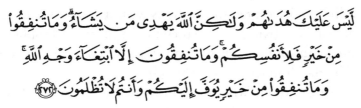

> In the beginning Muslims tended to hesitate in helping either their non-Muslim relatives or other non-Muslims who were in need.

> They thought that helping Muslims only constituted 'spending in the way of Allah'. This verse rejects this attitude… Muslims should not shrink from helping their relatives in the affairs of the world on the grounds that they are not following the true guidance; they will be rewarded by God for whatever help they render to needy persons for the sake of God.
>
> (*Towards Understanding the Qur'ān,* Vol.1, pp.211-12)

As regards social relations with non-Muslims, we are required to treat every human being with respect. We do not discriminate on account of anyone's faith or beliefs. The verse stating that the pagans are unclean (al-Tawbah 9: 28) only refers to their beliefs and does not indicate physical impurity. Thus if food which is not *ḥarām* is cooked by a non-Muslim and water is touched by him this does not render them unclean. Muslims can accept the invitation to share food with non-Muslims provided it is not *ḥarām*. The Qur'ān instructs Muslims to cooperate with others in activities that aim at the betterment of society (al-Mā'idah 5: 2). The exchange of gifts also helps to foster good relations. There are many instances recorded in *aḥādīth* that the Prophet sent gifts to non-Muslims and accepted their gifts as well. It is narrated by 'Alī ibn Abī Ṭālib that *Kisrā* (King of Iran) presented a gift to the Prophet, which he accepted and similarly gifts from Caesar and other kings were also accepted by the Prophet (*ṣaws*) (Aḥmad).

The question about whether non-Muslims are allowed to enter mosques is often raised. Most *fuqahā'* agree that only entering of the Grand Mosque in Makkah and surrounding *Ḥaram* as well as Masjid al-Nabawī in Madinah and its environs are prohibited to non-Muslims. As regards entering other mosques there is no such restriction.

We have seen that Islam exhorts its adherents to have cordial relations with non-Muslims. Then the question arises of how this can be reconciled with guidance given in the Qur'ān about avoiding close relations with them and confiding in them? For this purpose we have to understand the background against which such verses were revealed. It was the early Madinan period when non-believers, Jews and Christians, despite their differences were united in their opposition to the newly formed Islamic State. There was a constant state of war created by intrigues and conspiracies to topple or undermine Muslim rule. In this situation the Muslims were advised to remain firm in their *dīn* and be aware of the duplicity of hypocrites as they are more dangerous than their enemies. Thus the Muslims were warned to be on their guard against their enemies. In modern times, in a state of war nationals of belligerent powers are treated with suspicion and even imprisoned. When a state of war was over, Allah instructed the Muslims to have good relations with non-Muslims. Thus in *Sūrah al-Mumtaḥinah* after instructing Muslims not to befriend those who were inimical to the cause of Islam, the following verse states:

عَسَى ٱللَّهُ أَن يَجْعَلَ بَيْنَكُمْ وَبَيْنَ ٱلَّذِينَ عَادَيْتُم مِّنْهُم مَّوَدَّةً ۚ وَٱللَّهُ قَدِيرٌ ۚ وَٱللَّهُ غَفُورٌ
رَّحِيمٌ ﴿٧﴾ لَّا يَنْهَىٰكُمُ ٱللَّهُ عَنِ ٱلَّذِينَ لَمْ يُقَٰتِلُوكُمْ فِى ٱلدِّينِ وَلَمْ يُخْرِجُوكُم مِّن
دِيَٰرِكُمْ أَن تَبَرُّوهُمْ وَتُقْسِطُوٓا۟ إِلَيْهِمْ ۚ إِنَّ ٱللَّهَ يُحِبُّ ٱلْمُقْسِطِينَ ﴿٨﴾ إِنَّمَا يَنْهَىٰكُمُ
ٱللَّهُ عَنِ ٱلَّذِينَ قَٰتَلُوكُمْ فِى ٱلدِّينِ وَأَخْرَجُوكُم مِّن دِيَٰرِكُمْ وَظَٰهَرُوا۟ عَلَىٰٓ
إِخْرَاجِكُمْ أَن تَوَلَّوْهُمْ ۚ وَمَن يَتَوَلَّهُمْ فَأُو۟لَٰٓئِكَ هُمُ ٱلظَّٰلِمُونَ ﴿٩﴾

It may be that Allah will grant love (and friendship) between you and those whom you (now) hold as enemies. For Allah has power (over all things); and Allah is Oft-Forgiving, Most Merciful. Allah forbids you not, with regard to those who fight you not for (your) Faith nor drive you out of your homes, from dealing kindly and justly with them: for Allah loves those who are just. Allah only forbids you, with regard to those who fight you for (your) Faith, and drive you out of your homes, and support (others) in driving you out, from turning to them (for friendship and protection). It is such as turn to them (in these circumstances), that do wrong.

(al-Mumtaḥinah 60: 7-9)

These verses give very clear instructions for cultivating friendship and good relations with those who are not involved in any subversive or undermining activity against Islam. With these people we are instructed to be kind and just.

Let us pray that Allah (*swt*) may help us to convey the message of Islam wherever we live and that we treat all human beings kindly and justly.

(*Āmīn)*

Further Reading

- Syed Jalaluddin Umari: *Our Relationship with the Non-Muslims and Their Rights* [Urdu]. Aligarh: Idārah Taḥqīq wa Taṣnīf, 1999
- Atiq Ahmad Bastavi: 'Muslims in non-Muslim Countries' [Urdu]. *Bahthwa Naẓar*, Vol.13(4), 2001. pp.19-41

Terrorism

وَلَا تَبْغِ ٱلْفَسَادَ فِى ٱلْأَرْضِ ۖ إِنَّ ٱللَّهَ لَا يُحِبُّ ٱلْمُفْسِدِينَ ﴿٧٧﴾

And seek not (occasions for) mischief in the land: for Allah loves not those who do mischief.

(al-Qaṣaṣ 28: 77)

"The War on Terrorism" has become the slogan of the twenty-first century. Print and electronic media are saturated with news, views, comments, analysis and strategies to combat it. It seems everyone knows what terrorism is. But searching the literature for its definition is futile. Scholars say it is impossible to define. Even the General Assembly of the United Nations after considerable deliberations cannot come up with a definition of this widely used term. Thus, every nation or group or person defines it to suit its own interests. In other words it depends on the perspective of the person defining it. Terrorism is not a term that can be defined in a scientific way. It is an emotive and imprecise word. It is applied selectively for politically motivated violence of which we all disapprove. If this is the case then how can we judge what terrorism is? How can we distinguish wanton terrorism and the struggle for freedom in which oppressed people are engaged against state terrorism? Unfortunately oppressed Muslims in Palestine, Kashmir and Chechnya are struggling against the oppression perpetrated by Israel, India and the Russian Federation. Their just struggle is conveniently termed as terrorism and in the current debate Islam is linked with terrorism. It is being maligned as providing a haven for terrorists.

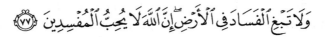

This is not a new accusation. Successive Western scholars have painted this violent picture of Islam for centuries. Norman Daniel after painstaking research has recorded: "The creation of a legend of Mohammed's life, violent and voluptuous, was an important part of Christian polemics" (*Islam and the West: Making of an Image*). So also R.W. Southern, a noted historian, confirmed: "This image of astonishing tenacity [about Islam] has changed very little from generation to generation" (*Views of Islam in the Middle Ages*). This image in spite of enlightenment and the development of secularism and humanism is part of the cultural mindset of the West today. Of course, there are reasons that have made this image perform new tasks in modern times. But let us examine the Islamic teachings about the inviolability of human life and respect for the rights of all human beings to live in peace and quiet.

In Islam the sanctity of human life is given paramount importance. Protection and respect for human life are the fundamental and basic teachings of Islam. This is accorded to all human beings alike. There is no distinction between Muslims and non-Muslims. The unjust killing of anyone violates the command of Allah. There are several verses in the Holy Qur'ān declaring this very clearly:

مَن قَتَلَ نَفْسًا بِغَيْرِ نَفْسٍ أَوْ فَسَادٍ فِى ٱلْأَرْضِ فَكَأَنَّمَا قَتَلَ ٱلنَّاسَ جَمِيعًا وَمَنْ أَحْيَاهَا فَكَأَنَّمَآ أَحْيَا ٱلنَّاسَ جَمِيعًا ... ﴿٣٢﴾

If anyone killed a person – unless it be a person guilty of manslaughter, or of spreading mischief in the land – it would be as if he killed the whole of mankind. And if anyone saved a life, it would be as if he saved the life of all human beings.

(al-Mā'idah 5: 32)

وَلَا تَقْتُلُواْ ٱلنَّفْسَ ٱلَّتِى حَرَّمَ ٱللَّهُ إِلَّا بِٱلْحَقِّ ... ﴿٣٣﴾

Do not kill any soul, whose killing has been forbidden by Allah, except for just cause.

(al-Isrā' 17: 33)

Abū Bakr Ṣiddīq, the First *Khalīfah* when sending his army on a mission instructed them: "Don't touch a woman, don't touch a child, an old man or a sick man. Don't burn a garden or harvest. Don't go on a scorcher policy." Thus, conquests were made with the minimum of bloodshed and cities were not razed to the ground nor reduced to rubble. 'Umar ibn al-Khaṭṭāb, the Second *Khalīfah* took the city of Jerusalem with the consent of the Christians without bloodshed. Later on Ṣalāḥuddīn Ayyūbī conquered Jerusalem and his guards kept order in every street and prevented violence. This does not mean that Muslims' conduct in the past and even today is without blemish.

Let us look at the record of those who accuse Islam and the Muslims of perpetrating terrorism. Leaving aside the barbaric atrocities of the crusaders and inquisitions in Europe involving the systematic killing and burning of people at the stake with a ferocity unknown to any beast, just consider the actions of the United States in the last century. The destruction of Hiroshima and Nagasaki by atomic bombs killing thousands of people and destroying the vegetation and making the land unfit for habitation for years are the worst terrorist acts ever committed. These were followed by other acts of American genocide which saw tens of thousands dead or maimed in Vietnam, Cambodia, Cuba, Chile, Iran, Greece, Nicaragua, Libya, Iraq, Sudan, Somalia, Afghanistan and Iraq. This list is very long indeed.

We all know that terrorist activities are taking place worldwide. Yet it is only the Muslims who are the target to be condemned and receive focused attention. There were terrorist activities going on in Northern Ireland for decades. The Tamil Tigers engaged in suicide bombings hold the world record for this. In Japan nerve gas attacks are still recent events. Yet all these events are explained away as grievances and mildly rebuked whereas the Muslims are singled out for special contempt and abuse. After the 11th September 2001 tragedy innocent Muslim citizens in the United States and Europe have been harassed, abused and detained without trial. This speaks volumes for the fairness and justice of human rights champions in the Western world.

So, how should we combat this terrorism menace? Like curing any other disease, physical or social, one has to look at its causes. Unless we try to eliminate the cause, superficial drastic action will not cure the disease. The war against terrorism like the war against poverty and crime requires actions that look at their causes and that we take appropriate action to eliminate them. For example to prevent crime we have to look at social conditions, unemployment, deprivation, bad housing, broken homes and many other social factors that create alienation from society and lead people to crime. Any amount of policing or harsh sentences will not help solve this problem. Similarly, we have to look at the causes which lead someone to blow themselves and others up. If people are desperate, imprisoned, tortured, denied human dignity and are oppressed and states use their full force to perpetuate this situation, no doubt people will take whatever action they can to highlight their grievances. Even the so-called superpowers instead of sympathising with the oppressed provide arms and moral support to the oppressors. So what sort of action is left to the oppressed?

قالَ رَسُولِ اللَّهِ صَلَّى اللَّهُ عَلَيْهِ وَسَلَّمَ انْصُرْ أَخَاكَ ظَالِمًا أَوْ مَظْلُومًا فَقَالَ رَجُلٌ يَا رَسُولَ اللَّهِ أَنْصُرُهُ إِذَا كَانَ مَظْلُومًا أَفَرَأَيْتَ إِذَا كَانَ ظَالِمًا كَيْفَ أَنْصُرُهُ قَالَ تَحْجُزُهُ أَوْ تَمْنَعُهُ مِنَ الظُّلْمِ فَإِنَّ ذَلِكَ نَصْرُهُ

(البخاري ومسلم)

The Prophet (*ṣaws*) once said: "Help your brother whether oppressor or oppressed." His Companions were taken aback and asked him: "We understand how to help the oppressed but how can we help the oppressor?" He replied: "By refraining him from oppression."

(Bukhārī and Muslim)

The Prophet (*ṣaws*) also gave a simile to illustrate the duty of people to refrain wrongdoers from their detrimental acts. He said that it is like some people travelling in a boat. There are passengers on the upper deck while others are on the lower. If passengers on the upper deck stop people of the lower deck drawing water from the sea for their use because it is inconvenient then some lower deck passengers will make a hole in the bottom of the boat to get their water requirements. After narrating this episode the Prophet (*ṣaws*) said:

فَإِنْ أَخَذُوا عَلَى يَدَيْهِ أَنْجَوْهُ وَنَجَّوْا أَنْفُسَهُمْ وَإِنْ تَرَكُوهُ
أَهْلَكُوهُ وَأَهْلَكُوا أَنْفُسَهُمْ

(البخاري)

If the passengers of the upper deck had held back those in the lower deck, they would have saved them as well as themselves. But if they had not stopped them from what they were doing and ignored their actions then they all would have drowned.

(Bukhārī)

The whole of humanity is now at sea and if we do not stop those who are rocking the boat we will all be destroyed.

There are nations in the world that hold 90 percent of the world's resources and they still want to dominate other nations in order to exploit their natural resources. The poor and desperate have no other option but to resort to violent acts. In order that they do not rock the boat they should be provided with help and support rather than exploiting and oppressing them further. What we need is not a new world order but a just world order, where people of the world can live in peace and prosperity. It is our duty to help the oppressors by preventing them from committing oppression. Only then can we get rid of the terrorism menace.

Let us pray that Allah, the Merciful and Beneficent, may make us work for world peace and help us to be the standardbearers of truth and justice.

(*Āmīn*)

Further Reading

- M.H. Syed (ed.): *Islamic Terrorism: Myth or Reality?* Delhi: Kalpaz Publ., 2002, 2 Vols.
- Khurram Murad: 'Islam and Terrorism'. *Encounters: Journal of Inter-Cultural Perspectives.* Vol. 4 (1) 1998
- Rahul Mahajan: 'The New Crusade: America's War on Terrorism'. New York: Monthly Review Press, 2002

Information Technology: Its Social and Moral Implications

اقْرَأْ وَرَبُّكَ الْأَكْرَمُ ﴿٣﴾ الَّذِي عَلَّمَ بِالْقَلَمِ ﴿٤﴾ عَلَّمَ الْإِنسَانَ مَا لَمْ يَعْلَمْ ﴿٥﴾

Recite! And your Lord is Most Bountiful, He Who taught (the use) of the pen – taught man that which he knew not.
(al-ʿAlaq 96: 3-5)

All natural resources are decreasing. Fossil fuels oil, coal and other resources are all heavily used by human beings and without adequate alternatives to replace them their stocks will exhaust. But information is one of the resources that is increasing manifold. And what we are experiencing is called the "information explosion". The expansion and progress in this field is happening at such a fast pace that it is difficult to keep up with all this IT – Information Technology. But there is not much thought given to its consequences for society. For example, how will this transform our lives? The revolution of which we are a part cannot be stopped and should not be. It will go on apace. It has enormous potential for good but at the same time it also poses very real and serious dangers. As Muslims we believe that all knowledge comes from Allah (*swt*). The verses from the very first revelation that I have just recited speak of the pen; the word processor is just its next stage of development. Knowledge is a useful tool but we also need guidance on how to use it properly. As Rūmī, a thirteenth-century Persian poet-philosopher said in his epic *Mathnawī*:

> If you acquire knowledge for your carnal self it is like a serpent.
> But if you seek it for your heart it is your friend.

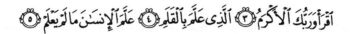

Thus, it is imperative for us to acquire this very useful and essential knowledge. But it is equally important to find a way that allows us to develop ourselves when using this technology.

IT raises many moral, social and political issues that we should address carefully. Of course, there are great benefits and much convenience provided by this tremendous tool we call the Internet. It is possible to search vast databases and retrieve useful references and even download full text as well. By the touch of a button you can tell the profitability of every company in the world, even that of any of its subsidiary companies as well. Through the Internet you can communicate to anybody in the world via an e-mail address. At the same time, with any human invention there are inherent dangers as well.

So what are the issues that we should consider about this very useful tool? As IT makes it easier to acquire and manipulate very useful information, it also makes it easier and simple to transfer pornography. Many chat lines encourage the exchange of lewd conversations and make people live in a virtual state of hypersexual excitement. Pornography has become a roaring business on the Internet. It is easy for anyone except the strong willed to be tempted by this means of sexual gratification. It also makes it possible for paedophiles and other perverts to exchange information and perpetrate their nefarious activities. They can also lure teenagers by posing as young people themselves: this in order to abuse them. Thus, we have to take very stringent actions to safeguard our society. While not infringing personal liberty we have a duty to protect ourselves from this exploitation. The World Wide Web is extensively used as a weapon to corrupt society. With the advance of technology it is now possible to penetrate our homes and reach young people without any censorship. Unless people apply self-restraint there is nothing to stop them from viewing and downloading pornography.

Then there are other social issues. If we examine the interplay between the social shaping of technology and the technological shaping of society, then we should endeavour to re-shape, re-direct or simply resist certain technological developments. We have to realise that technological developments and innovations are not in themselves there to shape our society. They have to be put in a social and cultural context and properly understood. We should constantly monitor, evaluate and justify the use of these very powerful forces and not just submit ourselves to its dictates.

Apart from these moral and social considerations there are many political concerns as well. The question one should ask is: who controls the information? The fact is that really rich and powerful organisations control the media. Whether it is the Murdoch Empire or CNN or even the BBC. They all have their own agenda. Theoretically, there is supposed to be the free flow of information. To be truly free, the information flow should be two-way, not simply in one direction.

However the concentration of the telecommunications industry, mass media outlets and data resources precludes a full flow of free and impartial information. Western media dominate and monopolise the distribution of news. The result is that stories written about Muslims and other developing countries are distributed and transmitted by international news agencies based in New York, London and Paris. Thus news about our neighbouring countries comes to us through foreign news media. Despite the claim of objectivity, the Western mass media often distorts news from the Third World. All of us have experienced listening to and viewing inaccuracies, slanted interpretations and untruths woven into news reports. These media moguls pour out what they want us to see and listen to. For example, from 1950 to 1989 the whole economy of the West was geared towards military expenditure to ward off the supposed threat from the Soviet Union. Billions of pounds were wasted on weapons. Scientists and technologists instead of using their resources for the betterment of mankind were engaged in the production of sophisticated arms and ammunitions. Now as the Red threat is no more it is being replaced by the threat of so-called Islamic fundamentalism. Islam is being portrayed as the great enemy of the West. The recent coverage of wars in Afghanistan and Iraq and the manipulation of the threat of weapons of mass destruction that led to them are the worst examples of news management. So how do we get our dissenting voices raised in the public domain?

A sample of distortion involves stressing bad news and ignoring good news. Powerful news outlets not only have the power to relay information, but they also have the power to ignore or censure information. For example, people can organise demonstrations and even collect millions of people to march on the streets of a capital city protesting against the government policy. Yet there may not be a single word of any speech on the radio or TV. This is known to have happened on many occasions. This conspiracy of silence is equally damaging. This power to ignore and to suppress information is something that should concern us all.

Another aspect for our consideration is cultural imperialism. It is now possible to transmit directly to all countries of the world. Western programmes and Western culture which only contaminate the elite in the Muslim world has now entered our drawing rooms and bedrooms with satellite dishes. This is something that no government can control. So how can we safeguard the vulnerable from this onslaught?

We should consider another aspect as well. Louis Joinet expressing his concern at a symposium on transborder data flow sponsored by the Organization of Economic Cooperation and Development said:

> Information is power and economic information is economic power. Information has an economic value, and ability to store and process certain types of data may well give one country political and technological advantage over other countries.

There is no control over what sort of data is collected by remote earth sensing satellites without permission. This again is loss of sovereignty and intrusion in the rights of states' resource management. There are many multinational organisations which collect and analyse data and exercise their propriety rights. There is no safeguard against this economic exploitation of poor countries.

Then governments and other organisations also collect personal information about people and without proper safeguards this information can be abused. They can even penetrate personal computers and extract data from them without the knowledge of their owners. George Orwell's scenario as depicted in his novel *1984* is not just fantasy. "Big Brother" is really watching us all. From sophisticated computer networks to grocery store checkout scanners, it is easier for governments, employers, advertisers and individuals to gather detailed personal information about each of us. Technological advances have made it possible for surveillance to become global and integrated – both commercial and government-related personal data flow across national boundaries and flow between private and public sectors as well. Thus we have to take measures to resist social control and incursions into our privacy.

We should be aware of these modern developments. We have to ask ourselves what systems do we need to achieve our objectives? Then we can develop our own databases and communication channels for dissemination of our message. We have to check that the information we get is accurate. So how can we establish the truth from the malicious lies? For this we have to think what organisations we need to secure our objectives. We have to learn to handle IT for the betterment of society. Thus, Information Technology has tremendous potential for both good and evil. It is our duty to channel it for the good of society. Following the guidance from our beloved Prophet (*ṣaws*) we should pray:

اَللّٰهُمَّ إِنِّي أَعُوذُ بِكَ مِنْ قَلْبٍ لاَ يَخْشَعُ وَمِنْ دُعَاءٍ لاَ يُسْمَعُ وَمِنْ نَفْسٍ لاَ تَشْبَعُ وَمِنْ عِلْمٍ لاَ يَنْفَعُ

(أحمد)

O My Lord! I seek Your refuge from a heart which is not fearful and the prayer which is not heard and the soul which is impatient and the knowledge which is not useful.

(Aḥmad)

اللّٰهُمَّ انْفَعْنِي بِمَا عَلَّمْتَنِي وَعَلِّمْنِي مَايَنْفَعُنِي وَزِدْنِي عِلْمًا

(الحاكم)

O My Lord! The knowledge that You have given me, make it useful to me. Only give me that knowledge which is useful to me and apportion me that knowledge which is beneficial, and increase my knowledge.

(Ḥākim)

We are all responsible for the knowledge which we acquire and we should use it for our benefit and for the benefit of mankind. May Allah (*swt*) guide us and help us in our efforts.

(*Āmīn*)

Further Reading:

- David Lyon: *The Information Society: Ideas and Illusions.* Cambridge: Polity Press, 1988
- David Lyon and Elia Zureik (eds.): *Computers, surveillance and privacy.* Minneapolis: University of Minnesota Press, 1996
- William James Stover: *Information Technology in the Third World: Can IT lead to Human National Development.* Boulder, Colorado: Westview, 1984

First *Khuṭbah*

الحَمْدُ لِلَّهِ نَحْمَدُهُ وَنَسْتَعِينُهُ وَنَسْتَغْفِرُهُ وَنُؤْمِنُ بِهِ وَنَتَوَكَّلُ عَلَيْهِ ـ وَنَعُوذُ بِاللَّهِ
مِنْ شُرُورِ أَنْفُسِنَا وَمِنْ سَيِّئَاتِ أَعْمَالِنَا ـ مَنْ يَهْدِهِ اللَّهُ فَلاَ مُضِلَّ لَهُ وَمَنْ
يُضْلِلْهُ فَلاَ هَادِيَ لَهُ ـ وَنَشْهَدُ أَنْ لاَ إِلَهَ إِلاَّ اللَّهُ وَحْدَهُ لاَ شَرِيْكَ لَهُ ـ
وَنَشْهَدُ أَنَّ مُحَمَّدًا عَبْدُهُ وَرَسُولُهُ ـ أَرْسَلَهُ بَشِيْرًا وَنَذِيرًا بَيْنَ يَدَي السَّاعَةِ ـ
مَنْ يُطِعِ اللَّهَ وَرَسُولَهُ فَقَدْ رَشَدَ وَاهْتَدَى، وَمَنْ يَعْصِهِمَا فَإِنَّهُ قَدْ غَوَى ـ وَإِنَّهُ
لاَيَضُرُّ إِلاَّ نَفْسَهُ وَلاَيَضُرُّ اللَّهَ شَيْئًا ـ إِنَّ خَيْرَ الحَدِيثِ كِتَابُ اللَّهِ وَخَيْرَ الهَدْيِ
هَدْيُ مُحَمَّدٍ صَلَّى اللَّهُ عَلَيْهِ وَسَلَّمَ، وَإِنَّ خَيْرَ الأُمُورِ عَوَازِمُهَا وَشَرَّ الأُمُورِ
مُحْدَثَاتُهَا، وَكُلُّ مُحْدَثَةٍ بِدْعَةٌ وَكُلُّ بِدْعَةٍ ضَلاَلَةٌ وَكُلُّ ضَلاَلَةٍ فِي النَّارِ.
أَمَّا بَعْدُ، فَأَعُوذُ بِاللهِ مِنَ الشَّيْطَانِ الرَّجِيمِ ـ بِسْمِ اللهِ الرَّحْمَنِ الرَّحِيمِ ـ
قَالَ اللهُ تَعَالَى فِي كِتَابِهِ الْمَجِيدِ ...*

Thankful praise be to Allah (*swt*). We thank and praise Allah seeking His help and His Forgiveness. We believe in Him and we have our trust in Him. We seek His refuge from the evil of our carnal selfs and from our sinful actions. Whomsoever Allah has guided no one can lead him astray and whomsoever Allah lets go astray no one can guide him. We bear witness that there is no deity except Allah and He is One and there are no partners with Him. We bear witness that Muḥammad is His servant and Messenger (peace be upon him). He was sent as a Bearer of glad tidings and as a Warner before the coming

* Please recite the *āyah* from the *Khuṭbah* you have chosen to deliver.

of the Hour. The one who obeys Allah and His Messenger is guided and achieves righteousness and he who disobeys them he has transgressed. He does not harm anyone but himself and he does not harm Allah at all. Certainly the best discourse is the Book of Allah and the best guidance is the guidance of Muḥammad. The peace and blessings of Allah be on him. The best deeds are firm and balanced acts and evil deeds are novel acts and new things introduced in the *dīn*. All novel acts are innovations and all innovations are spurious and misguided and all misguided are in the Fire.

I seek refuge with Allah from the accursed Satan. I begin in the Name of Allah, the Merciful, the Beneficent. *Allah Ta'ālā* says in His Glorious Book...**

** Please read the translation of the *āyah*.

Second *Khuṭbah*

الحَمْدُ لِلَّهِ رَبِّ العَالَمِينَ، وَالصَّــلاَةُ وَالسَّــلاَمُ عَلَى رَسُولِهِ الأَمِينِ، أَمَّا بَعْدُ: فَيَامَعْشَرَ الْمُسْلِمِينَ! أَعُوذُ بِاللَّهِ مِنَ الشَّيْطَانِ الرَّجِيمِ، بِسْمِ اللَّهِ الرَّحْمَنِ الرَّحِيمِ، قَالَ اللَّهُ تَعَالَى فِي كِتَابِهِ الكَرِيمِ: "إِنَّ اللَّهَ وَمَلاَئِكَتَهُ يُصَلُّونَ عَلَى النَّبِيِّ. يَاأَيُّهَا الَّذِيْنَ آمَنُوا صَلُّوا عَلَيْهِ وَسَلِّمُوا تَسْلِيمًا". اللَّهُمَّ صَــلِّ عَلَى سَــيِّدِنَا وَمَوْلاَنَا مُحَمَّدٍ بِعَدَدِ مَنْ صَلَّى وَصَامَ. اللَّهُمَّ صَلِّ عَلَى سَيِّدِنَا وَمَوْلاَنَا مُحَمَّدٍ بِعَدَدِ مَنْ قَعَدَ وَقَــامَ. اللَّهُمَّ صَلِّ عَلَى جَمِيعِ الأَنْبِيَاءِ وَالْمُرْسَلِينَ، وَعَلَى سَائِرِ الصَّحَابَةِ وَالتَّابِعِينَ، وَعَلَى عِبَادِكَ الصَّالِحِينَ. اللَّهُمَّ أَيِّدِ الإِسْلاَمَ وَالْمُسْلِمِينَ. اللَّهُمَّ اُنْصُرْ مَنْ نَصَرَ دِينَ مُحَمَّدٍ صَلَّى اللَّهُ عَلَيْهِ وَسَلَّمَ وَاجْعَلْنَا مِنْهُمْ، وَاخْذُلْ مَنْ خَذَلَ دِينَ مُحَمَّدٍ صَلَّى اللَّهُ عَلَيْهِ وَسَلَّمَ وَلاَتَجْعَلْنَا مِنْهُمْ. اللَّهُمَّ أَرِنَا الْحَقَّ حَقًّا وَارْزُقْنَا اتِّبَاعَهُ، وَأَرِنَا البَاطِلَ بَاطِلاً وَارْزُقْنَا اجْتِنَابَهُ. اللَّهُمَّ ثَبِّتْنَا عَلَى الإِسْلاَمِ. اللَّهُمَّ نَوِّرْ قُلُوبَنَا بِنُــورِ الإِيمَانِ. اللَّهُمَّ اغْفِرْ لِلْمُؤْمِنِــيْنَ وَالْمُؤْمِنَاتِ، الأَحْيَاءِ مِنْهُمْ وَالأَمْوَاتِ.

عِبَادَ اللَّهِ، رَحِمَكُمُ اللَّهُ، إِنَّ اللَّهَ يَأْمُرُ بِالعَدْلِ وَالإِحْسَانِ وَإِيتَاءِ ذِي القُرْبَى وَيَنْهَى عَنِ الفَحْشَاءِ وَالْمُنْكَرِ وَالبَغْيِ، يَعِظُكُمْ لَعَلَّكُم تَذَكَّرُونَ. اُذْكُرُوا اللَّهَ يَذْكُرْكُمْ، وَادْعُوهُ يَسْتَجِبْ لَكُمْ، وَلَذِكْرُ اللَّهِ تَعَالَى أَعْلَى وَأَوْلَى وَأَعَزُّ وَأَجَلُّ وَأَتَمُّ وَأَهَمُّ وَأَكْــبَرُ.

Praise be to Allah the Cherisher and Sustainer of the Worlds. Peace, blessings and salutations are on His Trustworthy Messenger. O Assembly of Muslims! I seek refuge with Allah from the accursed Satan. I begin in the name of Allah, the Merciful, the Beneficent. *Allah Taʿālā* has said in His Exalted Book: "Allah and His Angels send blessings on the Prophet: O you who believe send your blessings on him and salute him with respect." O Allah! Bless Our Master and Our Leader Prophet Muḥammad equal in number to those who pray and fast. O Allah! Bless Our Master and Our Leader Prophet Muḥammad equal in number to those who sit and stand. O Allah! Bless all Prophets and Messengers and bless all Companions and their successors and bless all Your pious servants. O Allah! Help those who help Islam and make us amongst them and forsake those who fail to help Islam and do not make us amongst them. O Allah! Show us the Truth as Truth and make us obey it and show us the Falsehood as Falsehood and save us from it. O Allah! Keep us steadfast in Islam. O Allah! Brighten our hearts with the light of *īmān*. O Allah! Forgive all believing men and women alive or dead.

Servants of Allah! May Allah have His Mercy on you. Allah commands justice, the doing of good, and liberality to kith and kin, and He forbids all shameful deeds, and injustice and rebellion: He instructs you that you may receive admonition. Remember Allah and He will remember you and pray to Him and He will respond. Remembrance of *Allah Taʿālā* is the Highest, the Foremost, the most Honourable, the Everlasting, the most Important and the Greatest.